Persiana

EVERYDAY

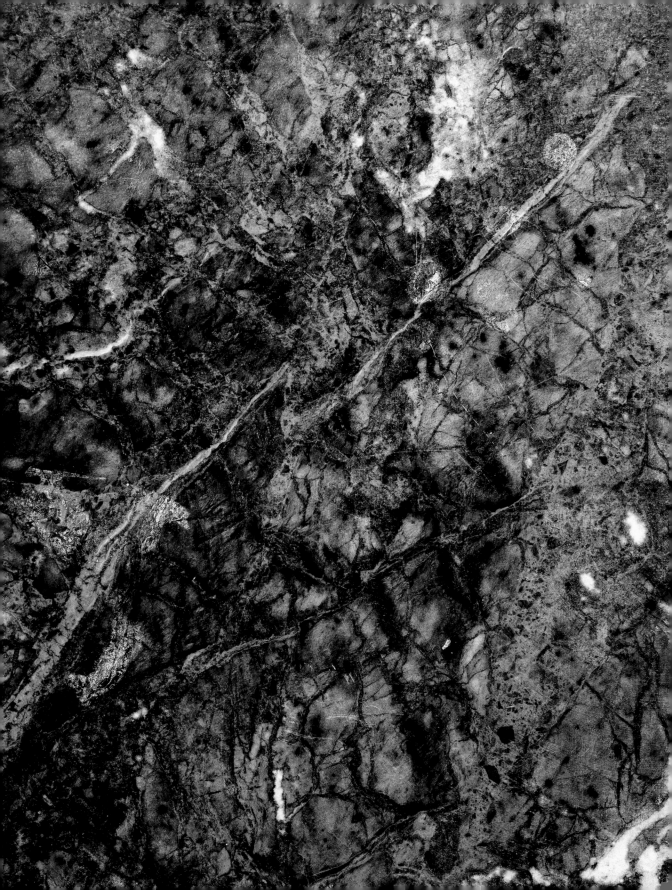

Persiana
EVERYDAY

SABRINA GHAYOUR

ASTER*

For my darling husband Stephen… chief taster, recipe guinea pig,
and all round wonderful human being. Even if your intense hatred
of all things cucumber is something I'll never fully understand,
I will love you with all my heart in this lifetime and the next.

CONTENTS

Introduction

Over the years I have had the good fortune of learning exactly what it is about my books and recipes that people seemed to value and enjoy so much, and easy, simple, quick, and delicious have always been the most popular feedback. Having considered the meaning of true simplicity and ease, I realized that many dishes I cook at home, and many ingredients and methods I use to "cheat" or make something simple, come naturally to me, and so might be of use to others too… and that's how this book was born.

If you are expecting all these recipes to take 15 minutes or have just 5 ingredients then I'm sorry to say I am not that girl. I don't like to conform to strict rules and by structuring recipes in a confined way I feel it can put pressure on home cooks who may be less confident, especially when it comes to experimenting and substituting ingredients. So this book may be a little different to other quick and easy cookbooks, but I can reassure you that I have included a great variety of no-cook recipes, one-pan and one-pot recipes, oven-baked recipes, quick-prep and slow-cook recipes, knock-out recipes for quick and easy vegetable dishes, plus plenty of vegan and vegetarian ideas to suit everyone. As always, I have embraced my store-cupboard ingredients and I love to use a lot of garlic granules, and even curry powder which has become a hero, to add depth and complexity of flavor to dishes.

When I wrote my first book *Persiana*, my aim was to cut through the mystery of Middle Eastern food by simplifying the cooking process and using ingredients that were readily available in supermarkets. Much to my surprise the book became a runaway success, and the ethos of simplicity has become my adopted style of cooking. "Persiana"—a word now synonymous with my culinary style—was merely my own nickname at the time, but it now stands for ease, reliability, and the exploration of flavors that perhaps, prior to the book's release in 2014, were unfamiliar and even a little daunting. Fast forward to today, these ingredients are now not only familiar, but are sold in every major supermarket and readily available for everyone to enjoy.

The pace at which Persian and Middle Eastern dishes and ingredients have gained popularity is incredible. Once perceived as a "trend," I'm proud that it is very much embedded in our culture due to some great chefs and cooks who have worked hard to champion this cuisine. This motivates me to keep experimenting to create recipes that are simple, flavorful, and economical.

I must confess that my life has changed since my previous book. I have become a wife and a stepmom to two boys, and this has been the greatest driving force behind creating this collection of recipes, as well as my ongoing desire to create flavourful, colourful feasts for my loved ones. I have now found that long, relaxing lunches and laid-back late dinners are no longer viable with a family to feed. Meals now have to be like clockwork on time, as well as quick, simple, crowd-pleasing, and plentiful. Since having a better understanding of families in similar situations, I knew it was the perfect time to write a collection of simple and straightforward recipes. Whether your time constraints are due to a busy family or simply due to life's demanding pace, you'll find recipes to suit a busy lifestyle in this book. Like all my recipes, the ingredients can be changed to suit your taste, and there are no hard and fast rules to follow unless I specifically say so in the recipe method.

All cooks, even the best ones, have fears when it comes to cooking, however, trust in me that I have tried to make this collection of recipes as easy and enjoyable as possible. After all, time is precious, and the less time you spend cooking, the more time you have to enjoy what you've cooked with friends and loved ones.

I hope this book ends up splattered, dog-eared and food-stained, because I have written it to be used every day. All the recipes I have shared in this book are dishes I make regularly at home, and I hope they inspire you to cook more often too.

Sabrina

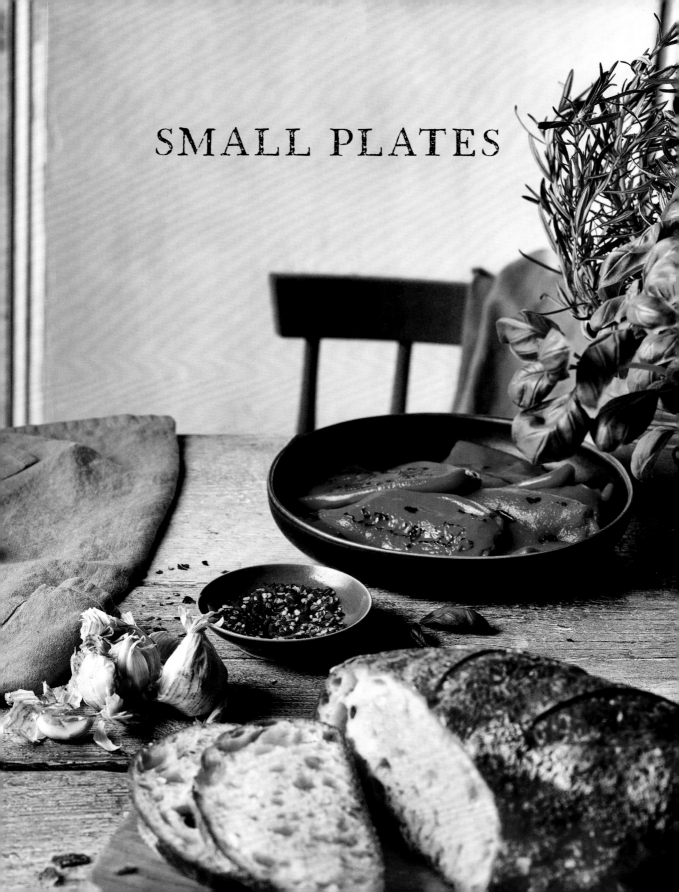

SMALL PLATES

My Muhammara

Although this is very different from any of the dips I usually make, it is utterly delicious. While the classic recipe uses walnuts, I prefer the robust crunch of roasted hazelnuts, and I like to cut corners by using ready-roasted bell peppers in brine. Not only can Muhammara be used as a dip, it's also great as a crostini topping or a sauce served either warm or cold, making it incredibly versatile. If you can't find chopped roasted hazelnuts, roast whole blanched hazelnuts in the oven preheated to 425°F, for 8 minutes, then let cool.

SERVES 4 TO 6

18oz jar roasted red peppers in brine

¾ cup chopped roasted hazelnuts

2 garlic cloves, finely minced

½ slice of white bread, torn into small chunks

3 tablespoons olive oil, plus extra for drizzling

1 teaspoon dried red chile flakes

juice of ½ lemon

1 small pack (about 1oz) of flat-leaf parsley, finely chopped

Maldon sea salt flakes and freshly ground black pepper

toasted bread or toasted mini pitta breads, to serve

Drain the roasted peppers well and then pat dry with paper towels to remove as much excess liquid as possible.

Put the hazelnuts, garlic, and peppers into a small food processor and blitz together. Add the bread, olive oil, chile flakes, and a generous amount of salt and pepper and blitz again until smooth.

Decant the mixture into a bowl, add the lemon juice and parsley, and mix well. Then adjust the seasoning to taste and drizzle with olive oil. Serve with some toasted bread or mini pittas.

SERVE WITH /// Fried Feta Parcels with Honey (see page 19) or Tahini, Citrus & Chicken Kebabs (see page 56).

Spiced mushroom loqmeh lettuce wraps
with yogurt & tamarind sauce

I am mad about lettuce wraps. They are such a great and simple way to pick up a delicious filling and bundle it into a hungry mouth. The filling here is meat-free but nevertheless delicious, and these *loqmeh* (rolled-up mouthfuls) are incredibly virtuous. Perfect if you want a little addition to a meal that won't upset the equilibrium of your other carefully planned dishes, or if you just want a light lunch or snack.

SERVES 2 TO 4

1lb 2oz cremino mushrooms, halved
  and thinly sliced

1 tablespoon garlic or olive oil

1 teaspoon ground cumin

1 teaspoon ground cinnamon

1 teaspoon paprika

1 teaspoon garlic granules

6 to 8 iceberg lettuce leaves, to use
  as wraps

⅓ cup thick Greek yogurt

4 teaspoons sweet tamarind sauce

2 to 3 teaspoons toasted sesame seeds

1 teaspoon pul biber chile flakes

Maldon sea salt flakes and freshly
  ground black pepper

pickled chilies, to serve

Heat a large over high heat and, once hot, add the mushrooms and dry-fry until all their liquid has been released and has evaporated.

Once the pan is dry again, add the oil and stir quickly to coat the mushrooms. Add all the spices, garlic granules, and a generous amount of salt and pepper and again stir quickly to coat the mushrooms and prevent the spices from burning. Remove from the heat.

Divide the mushroom mixture between the lettuce leaves. Dollop with the yogurt, drizzle with the tamarind sauce. Sprinkle with the sesame seeds, pul biber, top with pickled chiles, then serve immediately.

SERVE WITH /// Pomegranate Glazed Eggplant with Peanuts & Scallions (see page 134) or Spiced Lima Bean Patties (see page 136).

My ultimate tuna salad

I have an obsession with canned tuna that stems from my childhood. "Why on earth would you open a can of tuna, eat the contents, and then push the empty can under my cupboard?" were the words my mother repeated to me many a time. The truth is, I was a secret tuna-eater. I would come home from school, sneak into the kitchen, and pilfer a can of tuna, then devour the contents and hide the remaining evidence in Mom's bedroom. This is something I love and make a lot, and serve on hot toasted baguette or ciabatta slices as a lunch or light dinner, but it's equally good in flatbreads or wraps. It also makes a great topping for a baked potato, and can be used as a filling for a toasted sandwich with a little grated sharp Cheddar for a stunning tuna melt.

SERVES 3 TO 4

2 x 5oz cans tuna in oil

1 celery stalk, very finely diced

1 small red onion, very finely chopped

1 teaspoon dried red chile flakes

1 teaspoon nigella seeds

1 small pack (about 1oz) of fresh
  cilantro, very finely chopped

¼ to ⅓ cup mayonnaise

Maldon sea salt flakes and freshly
  ground black pepper

4 slices of toasted sourdough, to serve

Put all the ingredients into a mixing bowl with some salt and pepper and, using a fork, mix together until evenly combined. Taste to check the seasoning, and add more salt and pepper if desired.

Top the toasted sourdough with the tuna mixture and serve immediately.

SERVE WITH /// Zucchini, Apple, Peanut & Feta Salad (see page 46) or Golden Pepper, Cheese & Zucchini Kuku (see page 157).

Sweet & savory pastry twists

Cheese straws are such a party staple, and these are two of my favorite takes. Here are both sweet and savory options using the exact same method, giving you the perfect simple recipe to suit every mood and occasion.

MAKES 24

1 x 11oz ready-rolled puff pastry sheet (about 14 x 9½ inches)

1 egg, beaten

PARMESAN, FENNEL & BLACK PEPPER

1 heaped tablespoon fennel seeds

⅓ cup finely grated Parmesan cheese (or vegetarian alternative)

coarsely ground black pepper

PISTACHIO, CINNAMON & BROWN SUGAR

¼ cup demerara (or turbinado) sugar

1 teaspoon ground cinnamon

½ cup pistachio slivers (or whole unsalted nuts), finely chopped

Preheat the oven to 425°F. Line your largest baking pan with parchment paper.

Cut the pastry sheet lengthwise into 8 equal-sized strips. Cut each strip widthwise into 3 equal pieces, making a total of 24.

Brush all the strips with the beaten egg.

For the savory version, sprinkle the egg-washed pastry strips with the fennel seeds and Parmesan, and season well with coarsely ground pepper. Pat the toppings down firmly so they stick to the pastry.

Lift each strip and twist it, then place on the lined baking pan. Use any remaining beaten egg to brush over the exposed plain pastry in the center of the strips. Bake for 7 minutes, then let cool before serving.

For the sweet version, combine the sugar and cinnamon in a bowl, then sprinkle the mixture over the egg-washed pastry strips, followed by the pistachios. Pat the toppings down firmly before twisting and egg-washing the strips as above. Bake and cool as before.

SERVE WITH /// Butternut Soup Two Ways (see page 27) or Peanut Butter & Banana Soft-Serve (see page 225).

Fried feta parcels *with honey*

The first time I ate this dish was at a beautiful hotel on the beach in Kefalonia. I was so taken by the simplicity of it, but also inwardly angry at myself—number one fan of all things feta—that I hadn't thought of this combination myself. The only thing I have done differently from the hotel's version is to cut the feta block into four pieces rather than keeping it whole, so there is more pastry to enjoy. Either way, you'll be glad you made this, and if I could give you a piece of advice, keep some extra blocks of feta handy because you might want to use the rest of the filo pastry package to make more of these gorgeous parcels.

SERVES 2

vegetable oil, for frying

7oz block of feta cheese, cut into quarters

1 sheet of filo pastry (about 19 x 10 inches),
   cut into quarters

2 heaped tablespoons honey

Heat a skillet over medium heat, pour in about ½ inch of vegetable oil, and bring to a very low frying temperature. (Add a little piece of filo pastry. If it bubbles gently without sizzling too much, the oil is hot enough.)

Line a plate with a double layer of paper towels.

Wrap each rectangle of feta in a piece of filo and use a little oil or water to seal the seam on the underside.

Gently lay the parcels in the hot oil, seam-side down, and fry them for a couple of minutes until you see the pastry on the underside turn golden and bubble up a little. Then very carefully turn the parcels over and fry the other side until crisp and golden brown.

Remove from the pan with a slotted spoon and transfer to the paper-lined plate to drain, then serve on a plate drizzled with the honey.

SERVE WITH /// My Muhammara (see page 10) and Jeweled Tomato Salad (see page 53).

Ottoman puffs

I do love a classic sausage roll, and the less fussy and high-end the better. However, I also love flavor variations, and this recipe is an Eastern spin on the traditional approach. Studded with sharp barberries, herbs, and a little flourish of Turkish pul biber, the appearance of these puffs reminds me of little Ottoman pouffes. I defy you not to eat several straight from the oven.

MAKES 16

1 x 11oz ready-rolled puff pastry sheet (about 14 x 9 inches)
1 egg, beaten
1 tablespoon sesame seeds

For the filling

12oz sausagemeat
3 scallions, thinly sliced from root to tip
½ small pack (about ½oz) of dill, finely chopped
2 tablespoons dried barberries
1 teaspoon dried wild oregano
1 teaspoon garlic granules
1 teaspoon pul biber chile flakes
generous amount of Maldon sea salt flakes and freshly ground black pepper

Preheat the oven to 425°F. Line your largest baking pan with parchment paper.

Put all the filling ingredients into a mixing bowl and, using your hands, work them together really well for a couple of minutes until you have an evenly combined paste.

Cut the pastry lengthwise into 2 long strips. Divide the filling mixture in half and roll each half into an even sausage almost as long as the pastry strips. Lay a sausage down the center of each strip and fold the pastry edges over to enclose the sausage, brushing with a little beaten egg to seal.

Turn the rolls over, seam-side down, cut each one into 8 equal-sized pieces and place them on the lined pan. Brush all the exposed pastry with beaten egg and sprinkle with the sesame seeds, then bake for 22 to 25 minutes, until well browned and cooked through. Remove from oven, let cool slightly, and enjoy!

SERVE WITH /// Zucchini, Apple, Peanut & Feta Salad with Basil & Pul Biber (see page 46) or Golden Pepper, Cheese & Zucchini Kuku (see page 157).

Za'atar, tomato, olive & feta pastries

These lovely pastries are a wonderful savory indulgence of mine. I first made them in the 1990s when dried tomatoes became hugely trendy and were on every restaurant menu. Although less fashionable now, they remain a flavor bomb, adding instant impact to whatever they come in contact with. The blend of flavors here is almost Mediterranean and works really well with the crisp puff pastry. I like to let the pastries cool just a little before enjoying them, as they are best served warm.

MAKES 9

1 x 11oz ready-rolled puff pastry sheet (about 14 x 9 inches)

5½oz semi-dried tomatoes in oil

7oz feta cheese, crumbled

½ cup coarsely chopped Kalamata olives

2 tablespoons za'atar

freshly ground black pepper

Preheat the oven to 400°F. Line your largest baking pan with parchment paper.

Cut the pastry sheet into 3 vertically and horizontally to make 9 rectangles.

Drain the tomatoes and pat them dry with paper towels, then coarsely chop.

Mix the tomatoes with all the other ingredients in a mixing bowl, seasoning generously with pepper. Divide the mixture equally between each pastry rectangle, placing it in the center and patting flat.

Take 2 corners of the pastry rectangle and twist them together like a candy wrapper. Repeat with the 2 remaining corners, leaving the filling in the center exposed. Repeat with all the pastry rectangles.

Place the pastries on the lined baking pan and bake for 25 minutes, or until golden brown.

Remove from the oven and let cool slightly, then serve warm.

SERVE WITH /// Sticky Tamarind, Garlic & Tomato Green Beans (see page 172) or Butternut, Harissa & Coconut Soup (see page 28).

Zesty mackerel pâté

Smoked mackerel is such a great convenience food. Not only is it packed full of omega 3, but it's sold ready to eat everywhere. It's great with potatoes and other carbohydrates because its rich smoky flavor provides the perfect balance to simple flavors. This citrusy pâté is a great topping for toasted bread, and keeps well in the refrigerator for several days.

SERVES 4

10½oz smoked mackerel fillets (you can use plain or peppered fillets, as you prefer), skin removed

⅓ cup full-fat cream cheese

2 tablespoons horseradish cream

2 shallots, finely chopped

1 teaspoon pul biber chile flakes

finely grated zest of 1 small unwaxed orange and juice of ½ (use less juice if your orange is large)

1 small pack (about 1oz) of flat-leaf parsley, very finely chopped

handful of capers in brine, coarsely chopped

freshly ground black pepper (if using plain mackerel)

toasted tortillas or bread, to serve

Put the mackerel, cream cheese, and horseradish into small food processor and blitz until nice and smooth.

Transfer the mackerel mixture to a bowl, add all the other ingredients, seasoning generously with pepper only (as smoked mackerel is salty enough) if using plain mackerel, and stir well.

Decant the pâté into jars or ramekins and, if you have the time, refrigerate for at least an hour before serving with toasted tortillas.

SERVE WITH /// Yogurt, Marjoram & Pul Biber Flatbreads (see page 209).

Butternut soup two ways

BUTTERNUT, CARDAMOM & TAHINI SOUP

Butternut squash is a staple in my house, and here it makes a beautifully smooth and fragrant soup. The gently aromatic spicing works perfectly with the sweetness of butternut, and the tahini gives it wonderful body. Tahini can be used to add a layer of depth and richness to all manner of vegan soups and stews, enriching them in a way that only dairy and meat otherwise would. This is a really good, quick, and easy recipe for simple soup satisfaction.

SERVES 4 TO 6

olive oil

1 large onion, coarsely chopped

2¼ to 2¾lb butternut squash, peeled, seeded, and cut into 1-inch cubes

1 teaspoon ground turmeric

1 teaspoon ground cumin

seeds from 4 large green cardamom pods, ground using a mortar and pestle

1 teaspoon garlic granules

2 heaped tablespoons tahini

generous squeeze of lemon juice

Maldon sea salt flakes and freshly ground black pepper

Place a large saucepan over medium heat and pour in just enough olive oil to just coat the bottom. Add the onion and cook until softened and translucent. Then add the butternut pieces, all the ground spices, the garlic granules, and a generous amount of salt and pepper, and stir thoroughly for 5–6 minutes to coat the butternut in the spices.

Add enough boiling water to just about cover the ingredients, stir, and then cover the pan with a lid. Reduce the heat a little and simmer for 35 to 40 minutes, until the butternut pieces are soft and almost mashable with a fork.

Using a hand-held stick blender, blitz the soup until smooth. Add the tahini with the lemon juice and stir thoroughly until dissolved. Check and adjust the seasoning to taste before serving.

SERVE WITH /// Parmesan, Fennel & Black Pepper Pastry Twists (see page 16) or Yogurt, Marjoram & Pul Biber Flatbreads (see page 209).

BUTTERNUT, HARISSA & COCONUT SOUP

With its creamy coconut flavor, this recipe feels almost Thai in style. The harissa gives a depth of heat and flavor that is different from chiles on their own, and the heat is perfectly balanced by the sweet nature of the butternut.

SERVES 4 TO 6

2 tablespoons olive oil

1 large onion, coarsely chopped

3½lb butternut squash, peeled, seeded,
   and cut into 1-inch cubes

2 heaped tablespoons rose harissa

1 teaspoon garlic granules

1 teaspoon curry powder

generous squeeze of lemon or lime juice

14oz can full-fat coconut milk

Maldon sea salt flakes and freshly ground
   black pepper

bread, to serve

Place a large saucepan over medium heat and pour in the olive oil. Add the onion and cook until beginning to soften but without coloring. Then add the cubed squash, stir to coat in the onion mixture, and cook for 5 minutes or so until the edges begin to soften. Add the harissa, garlic granules, curry powder, and a generous amount of salt and pepper, and stir thoroughly to coat the squash in the harissa.

Add enough boiling water to almost cover the ingredients, then stir and cover the pan with a lid. Reduce the heat a little and simmer for 25 minutes, or until the squash cubes are soft and almost mashable with a fork. Remove the pan from the heat.

Using a hand-held stick blender, blitz the soup until smooth. Add the lemon or lime juice and adjust the seasoning to taste. Stir in the coconut milk, place the soup back on the heat, and reduce to your desired thickness before serving.

SERVE WITH /// Cheese, Thyme & Walnut Flatbreads with Honey (see page 189) or Za'atar, Tomato, Olive & Feta Pastries (see page 22).

Halloumi, bacon, date & apple salad

Devils on horseback was a 1970s party staple of prunes wrapped in bacon, and as a kid I absolutely loved them. This was also the source of my long-standing love for all things salty and sweet combined. Here, I've added halloumi into the equation and changed the prunes to dates for a fresh twist on the classic bite.

SERVES 4

9oz block of halloumi cheese

8 strips smoked bacon

4 large Medjool dates, pitted
and halved

For the salad

2 tablespoons olive oil

1 tablespoon red wine vinegar

1 tablespoon honey

1 teaspoon ground cinnamon

1 teaspoon water

handful of mixed salad leaves

1 apple, cored and sliced (I like
Braeburn)

Preheat your oven to its highest setting 15 to 20 minutes before you start cooking. Line a large baking pan with parchment paper.

While the oven is heating up, cut the block of halloumi in half lengthwise so you have two long rectangular pieces, then cut each piece into 4 equal fingers.

Lay a strip of bacon on your work surface and place a finger of halloumi across it at one end. Set half a date on top of the halloumi. Roll the halloumi and date tightly in the bacon until you have a neat bundle. Repeat with the remaining ingredients, then place the bundles on the lined baking pan.

Roast the bundles for 10 to 12 minutes until the bacon is really crisp all over.

Meanwhile, for the salad, put the olive oil, vinegar, honey, cinnamon, and water in a small bowl and mix together until well combined. Put the mixed leaves in a serving dish, drizzle with the dressing, and scatter with the apple slices.

Remove the bundles from the oven and serve with the salad.

SERVE WITH /// Cumin & Lemon Asparagus (see page 149) or Super-Quick Smoky Tomato Couscous (see page 199).

Baked halloumi *with lemon, wild thyme & honey*

Baked halloumi is a thing of beauty. Don't believe me? Just try the baked halloumi recipe from my fourth book, *Bazaar*. These days I tend to have a no-rules approach to baking halloumi and find that the "anything goes" vibe works very well. Truth be told, halloumi is ideally suited to bold flavors, punchy herbs, and aromatics, and this combo fulfills my insatiable desire for all things salty, sweet, hot, and sour. Try it, and have some bread ready on the side.

SERVES 2 TO 4

9oz block of halloumi cheese

2 tablespoons garlic oil

1 heaped tablespoon honey

finely grated zest of 1 large unwaxed
  lemon and juice of ½

1 teaspoon dried wild thyme

½ teaspoon coarsely ground black pepper

1 teaspoon pul biber chile flakes

flatbread, to serve

Preheat the oven to 425°F. Set out a square of foil large enough to generously accommodate the block of halloumi, line it with a square of parchment paper, and place the halloumi in the center. Crumple the paper tightly around the block, leaving only the top surface exposed.

Mix all the other ingredients together in a small bowl until evenly combined, then pour over the halloumi.

Crumple the foil around the halloumi to form a sealed parcel. Place in a small ovenproof dish or on a baking pan and bake for 30 minutes.

Remove from the oven and serve immediately with flatbread.

SERVE WITH /// Za'atar, Paprika & Garlic Chicken (see page 72) or Lamb & Eggplant Kebabs (see page 106).

My flavor bomb beans on toast

Deeply flavorsome, rich and satisfying, this is next-level beans on toast and versatile enough that you could make a brunch by cracking eggs into it. 'Nduja is one of my favorite flavor bombs to keep in the larder, the supremely spicy, spreadable Calabrian pork salami that melts when you expose it to heat and enriches anything it touches. It's the perfect partner for beans, and its spiciness means it can stand up to the boldness of the fennel and cumin too.

MAKES 2

½ teaspoon cumin seeds

½ teaspoon fennel seeds

2 generous pinches of Maldon
   sea salt flakes

2½oz 'nduja

5 sprigs of oregano, leaves picked

3 large tomatoes, cored and
   coarsely chopped

14oz can black-eye beans, drained

2 tablespoons butter

2 slices of toasted sourdough,
   to serve

Heat a large, dry skillet over medium-high heat, add the cumin and fennel seeds, and dry-toast for about a minute, or until they release their aroma, shaking the pan intermittently to prevent them from burning.

Transfer the toasted seeds to a mortar, add the salt, and use the pestle to grind to a coarse consistency.

Add the 'nduja to the skillet and begin breaking it down immediately. As it warms up, it will soften within a couple of minutes. Once soft, add the spiced salt and the oregano leaves and stir well. Add the tomatoes, stir, and cook for 3 to 4 minutes.

Add the beans and stir to coat them well in the tomato mixture, then let cook for 3 to 4 minutes until they are nice and hot. Add the butter, let it melt, and then stir into the bean mixture.

Pile the beans onto the toasted sourdough and serve immediately. This needs no accompaniment.

SALADS FOR ALL SEASONS

Fennel, feta, orange & pistachio salad

Sometimes when you are roasting meats or perhaps creating a series of rich dishes, you want a single salad that will refresh the palate beautifully and provide you with the right kind of flavor to pair with almost anything. This is exactly that salad, and the combination of ingredients is just as wonderful as an accompaniment to meatless dishes, such as stews, pies, and quiches. I don't mind admitting that it's rather pretty, too!

SERVES 4 TO 6

2 oranges

1 large fennel bulb, trimmed, quartered,
   and shaved or very thinly sliced,
    fronds reserved

3½oz feta cheese

½ cup pomegranate seeds

olive oil, for drizzling

⅓ cup coarsely chopped pistachio nuts

teaspoon pul biber chile flakes

Maldon sea salt flakes and freshly
   ground pepper

Using a sharp knife, cut a disk of peel off the top and bottom of each orange, then, working from the top of the fruit downward, cut away the remaining peel and pith in strips, just enough to expose the orange flesh, until the entire orange is peeled. Cut each orange in half widthwise, then cut each half into about 5 half-moon slices.

Arrange the fennel on a platter, add the oranges, and season generously with salt and pepper. Crumble the feta over the salad, sprinkle with the pomegranate seeds and fennel fronds, and drizzle with a little olive oil.

Scatter with the pistachios and finally sprinkle with the pul biber and then serve.

SERVE WITH /// Harissa & Lemon Roasted Chicken Thighs (see page 58) or Bloody Mary Spatchcocked Chicken (see page 80).

Chicken & cucumber salad
with pul biber & tahini lime dressing

Although I love salads, for me they need to have bags of flavor and tick many boxes. Fresh, zingy, crunchy, sometimes sweet and spicy, I always need a salad to be a filling meal in its own right. This stunner using leftover chicken is a nod to chicken satay salads but using the Middle Eastern staples of tahini and cucumber, and we Persians have an unhealthy obsession with cucumber! It really is refreshing and full of flavor. Perfect for sharing, or not…

SERVES 2 TO 4

1 large cucumber, peeled and cut into thin batons or strips using a vegetable peeler

2 cooked chicken breasts, shredded (or use chicken thighs or drumsticks)

3 scallions, thinly sliced diagonally from root to tip

1 teaspoon pul biber chile flakes

handful of salted peanuts or cashews

handful of fresh cilantro leaves

Maldon sea salt flakes and freshly ground black pepper

For the dressing

1 heaped tablespoon tahini

juice of 1 lime

1 tablespoon light soy sauce

1 heaped teaspoon honey

Arrange the cucumber, chicken, and scallions on a large platter and season with a little salt and pepper.

Mix all the dressing ingredients together in a small bowl and drizzle over the salad.

Sprinkle with the pul biber, scatter with the nuts and cilantro leaves, and serve. This needs no accompaniment.

Bazaar spiced chickpea & feta salad

Chickpeas are a fantastic staple for me. From using them to make falafels and soups and stews to roasting them as snacks or mashing them with spices and cheese as a sandwich filling, I've covered every angle in my recipes. They are also ideal for making quick salads, being great carriers of flavor. This vibrant and delicious example can be thrown together in minutes, perfect for a meal in a pinch or for adding a little extra pizzazz to a feast.

SERVES 4

14oz can chickpeas, drained

4 sprigs of mint, leaves picked, rolled up tightly and cut into ribbons

4 sprigs of basil, leaves picked, rolled up tightly and cut into ribbons

4 scallions, thinly sliced from root to tip

3½oz feta cheese, crumbled

½ cup pomegranate seeds

For the dressing

2 tablespoons extra virgin olive oil

juice of ½ lemon

1 teaspoon honey

1 heaped teaspoon sumac

½ teaspoon ground cumin

½ teaspoon ground cinnamon

Maldon sea salt flakes and freshly ground black pepper

Put all the ingredients for the salad into a bowl and toss together.

Mix all the dressing ingredients together in a small pitcher or bowl until evenly combined, seasoning well with salt and pepper.

Pour the dressing over the salad and toss again. Serve at room temperature.

SERVE WITH /// Three Ways with Chicken (see page 64) or Fast & Slow Souk-Spiced Leg of Lamb (see page 95).

Seared pepper steak & tomato salad
with sweet & spicy lime dressing

Ever since I first visited Thailand back in 2009, I've had a thing for steak salad that I can't quite explain. While this version is quite different, I think it might be the house favorite now, as the dressing is "just right" and seems to hit the spot with everyone.

SERVES 1 TO 2

1 sirloin steak, about 9oz

very generous amount of coarsely ground black pepper (enough to heavily season both sides of the steak)

2 tablespoons olive oil

1 tablespoon light soy sauce

1 tablespoon superfine sugar

finely grated zest and juice of 1 unwaxed lime

1 teaspoon pul biber chile flakes

7oz baby tomatoes (preferably multicolored)

2 scallions, thinly sliced from root to tip

handful of fresh cilantro leaves

sprinkling of black sesame seeds (optional)

Coat the steak on both sides with the coarsely ground pepper and press down to help the pepper stick.

Heat a skillet over high heat and, once it is super-hot, drizzle 1 tablespoon olive oil equally over both sides of the steak. Sear it for 2 to 3 minutes on each side until a deep crust forms.

Remove from the pan and let rest, covered in foil, for 5 minutes.

Mix together the remaining olive oil, the soy sauce, sugar, lime zest and juice, and the pul biber in a bowl, then add the tomatoes and scallions and toss until well dressed.

Once the steak has rested, slice widthwise into thin strips and arrange on a plate. Scatter the steak with the tomatoes and scallions, and then drizzle evenly with the dressing. Scatter with the cilantro leaves, and sesame seeds if you like, and serve.

SERVE WITH /// Pomegranate Glazed Eggplant with Peanuts & Scallions (see page 134) or Cumin & Lemon Asparagus (see page 149).

Zucchini, apple, peanut & feta salad
with basil & pul biber

Crunchy, fresh, sweet, and salty, this is another winner of a salad that is simple to cobble together, with the apple really making its mark. I never thought I would pair zucchini and apple in a recipe, but it works. Not only quick and easy, the salad looks beautiful to boot.

SERVES 2 TO 4

1 large zucchini

1 apple (I like Braeburn)

2½oz feta cheese

about 1 tablespoon or so olive oil

generous squeeze of lemon juice

generous handful of salted peanuts,
    coarsely chopped

generous handful of basil leaves,
    rolled up tightly and thinly sliced
    into ribbons

2 pinches of pul biber chile flakes

Maldon sea salt flakes and freshly
    ground black pepper

Using a vegetable peeler, carefully peel long, wide strips down the length of the zucchini, then arrange them on a platter.

Quarter and core the apple, then thinly slice the quarters into half-moons. Lay these on top of the zucchini.

Crumble the feta cheese over the salad, then season with salt and pepper (go heavy on the pepper), drizzle with the olive oil, and squeeze over the lemon juice. Lastly, scatter with the peanuts, basil, and the pul biber and serve.

SERVE WITH /// My Ultimate Tuna Salad (see page 15) or Ottoman Puffs (see page 20).

Fig, beet, goat cheese, red chile & walnut salad

I really do love the ingredients in this salad so much. While beet and goat cheese is a classic salad pairing, if the dressing isn't right, it can be somewhat lackluster and in need of a little sparkle. Adding figs gives it not only a lovely sweetness but a pleasing texture, and the red chile and walnuts work with all the ingredients beautifully, so no additional seasoning required. Best part? I always have vacuum-packed beets in my refrigerator to rescue me when ingredients are a bit thin on the ground and I'm not feeling terribly inspired.

SERVES 4 TO 6

3oz arugula leaves

4 large black or green figs, quartered

9oz vacuum-packed cooked beets in natural juice (or 4 small peeled, cooked whole fresh beets), quartered

7oz rindless soft goat cheese

½ cup coarsely broken walnut halves

1 long red chile, seeded and very finely chopped

For the dressing

3 tablespoons pomegranate molasses

1 heaped tablespoon honey

1 tablespoon white wine vinegar

1 tablespoon olive oil

Mix all the dressing ingredients together in a small pitcher or bowl until evenly combined.

Select a large platter and arrange the arugula on it, followed by the fig and beet quarters. Break the goat cheese into small pieces and dot all over the salad.

Drizzle the salad with the dressing, scatter with the walnuts and chopped chile, and serve immediately.

SERVE WITH /// Tahini, Citrus, Chicken Kebabs (see page 56) or Lamb Chops with Yogurt, Fenugreek & Herbs (see page 109).

Georgian kidney bean salad

This is my nod to a Georgian *lobio* (bean) salad. We Persians are great lovers of legumes of all kinds, and much like Persians, Georgians use an abundance of herbs in their recipes, which perhaps explains my gravitation toward this dish. Kidney beans are exceptionally sweet, so the addition of onions and some pul biber strike the perfect balance to finish off this lovely salad and make it a real winner.

SERVES 6 TO 8

2 x 14oz cans kidney beans

1 cup coarsely chopped flat-leaf parsley

2 heaped teaspoons dried mint

2 long (banana) shallots, very thinly sliced
   into rings

2 tablespoons vegan red wine vinegar

2 tablespoons olive oil

2 teaspoons pul biber chile flakes

Maldon sea salt flakes and freshly ground
   black pepper

Tip the cans of beans into a sieve and rinse off any excess starch and brine, then shake dry and tip them into a mixing bowl.

Add all the other ingredients to the bowl and fold together carefully to ensure you don't crush the beans. Season generously with salt and pepper, stir again, and let rest at room temperature for 20 to 30 minutes so the dressing can soak into the beans.

Stir well again before serving.

SERVE WITH /// Pork, Cilantro & Scallion Meatballs (see page 61) or Sesame & Spice-Roasted Salmon (see page 119).

Jeweled tomato salad

Tomato salads are probably my favorite of all salads. Nothing satisfies more than juicy, sweet, ripe tomatoes. But sometimes even when they aren't ripe or in season, a few ingredients and the right dressing can really help bring the flavors together and elevate the humble tomato into something rather more grand. While the tomatoes themselves are the star of the show, I love the wonderful pomegranate, olive, and pistachio jewels that stud this salad and really bring it to life.

SERVES 4

14oz baby tomatoes (multicolored if possible)

2 long (banana) shallots, thinly sliced into rings

2 handfuls of your favorite olives, pitted

½ cup pomegranate seeds

large handful of mint leaves, rolled up tightly and cut into ribbons

large handful of fresh cilantro leaves, torn

generous handful of pistachio nuts, coarsely chopped

Maldon sea salt flakes and freshly ground black pepper

For the dressing

2 tablespoons olive oil

1 heaped tablespoon date molasses

1 tablespoon vegan red wine vinegar

Put all the ingredients for the salad into a bowl, season generously with salt and pepper, and toss together lightly.

Mix the dressing ingredients together in a small pitcher or bowl until evenly combined.

Pour the dressing over the salad and toss again, then serve.

SERVE WITH /// Fried Feta Parcels with Honey (see page 19) or Fast & Slow Souk-Spiced Leg of Lamb (see page 95).

POULTRY
& MEAT

Tahini, citrus, chicken kebabs

This is an old recipe I used when I first started teaching cooking classes,. Back then, many folks didn't know how to use tahini other than in hummus and maybe the odd sauce here and there. Even now, I think it's worthy of wider use. The marinade here has a wonderful nutty flavour from its sesame base, the warmth of garlic and the sumac adds a lovely citrus flourish.

SERVES 4 TO 6

1¼lb chicken mini tenders

vegetable oil, for frying

For the marinade

¼ cup tahini

2 tablespoons Greek yogurt

2 tablespoons olive oil

2 tablespoons sumac

1 heaped teaspoon garlic granules

2 fat garlic cloves, crushed

1 small pack (about 1oz) of fresh cilantro, finely chopped

finely grated zest and juice of 1 unwaxed lemon

finely grated zest and juice of 1 unwaxed orange

generous amount of Maldon sea salt and freshly ground black pepper

To serve

tortillas or flatbreads

thinly sliced red onion

cilantro and mint leaves

Greek yogurt

Mix all the marinade ingredients together in a wide, shallow nonreactive dish until well combined. Add the chicken tenders and turn until well coated in the marinade. Cover the dish with plastic wrap and let marinate at room temperature for at least 30 minutes. You can cook them immediately, but a little marinating time will allow the flavors to permeate the chicken surface. The marinade contains acid (lemon juice), so I would not recommend marinating them for longer than a few hours.

When you are ready to fry, heat a large skillet over medium-high heat and add a good drizzle of vegetable oil. Once hot, shake the excess marinade off the chicken tenders one at a time and add to the skillet. Do this in batches, if necessary, to avoid overcrowding the pan, and cook for 3 to 4 minutes on one side, then turn and cook for 1 to 2 minutes on the other side (the exact cooking time will vary depending on the size of the tenders, so keep an eye on them). I like to serve these kebabs on skewers alongside tortillas, Greek yogurt, sliced red onion, cilantro and mint leaves.

SERVE WITH /// My Muhammara (see page 10) or Fig, Beet, Goat Cheese, Red Chile & Walnut Salad (see page 48).

Harissa & lemon roasted chicken thighs

This is such a simple recipe that I confess I have been making it for years and never thought to put it in one of my books. It's so handy and versatile, as it can be sliced and stuffed into wraps or pitta bread for lunchboxes, shredded and added to salads, or used in stir-fries or rice noodle dishes. But it also pairs perfectly with steamed rice or naan in the same way tandoori chicken does. You can also marinate the chicken up to 48 hours in advance, or freeze the marinated raw chicken for use at a later date or for batch cooking.

SERVES 4 TO 6

2¼lb boneless, skinless chicken thighs

2 heaped tablespoons rose harissa

⅔ cup Greek yogurt, plus extra for
    serving

finely grated zest and juice of
    1 unwaxed lemon

Maldon sea salt flakes and freshly
    ground black pepper

To serve (optional)

flatbreads or tortillas

cilantro leaves

thinly sliced scallions

lemon wedges

Preheat the oven to 500°F. Line a baking pan with parchment paper.

Put the chicken thighs into a mixing bowl, add the other ingredients with a generous amount of salt and pepper, and roll the chicken over to coat well in the mixture, preferably using your hands.

Lay the chicken thighs on the lined pan and roast for 40 minutes or until sticky and charred around the edges and cooked through.

To serve, slice the chicken and serve in warmed flatbreads with Greek yogurt, cilantro leaves, sliced scallions, and alongside lemon wedges for squeezing over.

SERVE WITH /// Fennel, Feta, Orange & Pistachio Salad (see page 39) or Three Simple Ways With Rice (see page 192).

Pork, cilantro & scallion meatballs
with tamarind glaze

Meatballs are an easy dish to put together, and the sticky sweet and sour glaze on these makes them ever so moreish. To eat them *banh mi*-style, serve the meatballs in a baguette with a little quick-pickled onion and carrot (make your own by mixing salt with a little superfine sugar and some rice vinegar in a lidded container, add thinly sliced onion and carrot, and shake for a couple of minutes).

MAKES
20 TO 22
MEATBALLS

1lb 2oz ground pork (15 to 20% fat)
1 bunch of scallions, very thinly sliced
    from root to tip
1 tablespoon garlic granules
1 teaspoon ground white pepper
1 small pack (about 1oz) of fresh
    cilantro, very finely chopped,
    plus extra to serve
3 tablespoons honey
Maldon sea salt flakes

3 tablespoons unsweetened
    tamarind paste (I used a lighter,
    less concentrated one)

To serve (optional)
baguettes
finely chopped fresh red chile
quick pickled onion and carrot
    (see above)

Preheat the oven to 425°F. Line a baking pan with parchment paper.

Put the ground pork, scallions, garlic granules, white pepper, cilantro, and a generous amount of salt into a mixing bowl. Using your hands, work them together until you have an evenly combined paste.

Mix the tamarind and honey together in a small bowl and taste to ensure it is a nice balance of sweet and sour. Every tamarind paste will differ, so you might need to adjust the quantities a little.

Roll the meat mixture into approximately 1-inch balls, making about 20 to 22 in total (to be as precise as possible, if you have kitchen scales, you can weigh the mixture and divide it up), and place on the lined pan.

Roast the meatballs for 25 minutes. Shake the pan to loosen them, then drizzle them with the tamarind and honey mixture. Using a spatula, coat the meatballs in the glaze as best you can, shaking the pan too, if necessary, then roast for another 10 minutes.

Remove from the oven, shake the meatballs once more to roll them through the sticky glaze. Serve in baguettes with cilantro, finely chopped red chile, and pickled onion and carrot.

SERVE WITH /// Georgian Kidney Bean Salad (see page 50) or Three Simple Ways With Rice (see page 192).

Aromatic spiced beef & tomato polow
with peas

One-pot cooking is the savior of so many occasions when I just don't have the time or energy to do more than that. This is a winner. Tried and tested on my biggest critics (my stepsons), it garnered a massive thumbs-up. With so much going for it, this really needs no accompaniment whatsoever. It's just the ticket when you want to feed a hungry mob quickly and economically. While I've used beef here, ground lamb, pork, turkey, or chicken also work well. Being Persian, I love this served with some plain yogurt on the side, but it must be said, kids (of all ages, it seems) love it with ketchup, too. What can you do, eh?

SERVES 4 TO 6

olive or vegetable oil

1 large onion, finely chopped

1lb 2oz ground beef

3 heaped tablespoons tomato paste

2 tablespoons curry powder

1 teaspoon ground cinnamon

1 teaspoon ground cumin

½ teaspoon dried red chile flakes

3 to 4 bay leaves

4 fat garlic cloves, thinly sliced

2 handfuls of frozen peas

2 cups basmati rice

2 tablespoons butter

3 cups cold water

plain yogurt, to serve

Maldon sea salt flakes and freshly
   ground black pepper

Select a large skillet with deep sides and as well as a lid, or use a large saucepan. Place over medium-high heat and drizzle in a little oil. Add the onion and cook until soft and translucent.

Add the ground beef and immediately break it up as finely as you can to prevent it from cooking in clumps. While still uncooked, add the tomato paste, all the spices and bay leaves, and stir to coat the meat well. Add the garlic, peas, and a *very* generous amount of salt and pepper (as you are seasoning a whole skillet of rice), then add the rice and butter. Stir all the ingredients together until the butter has melted and blended in.

Pour in the cold water, cover the skillet, and cook on very low heat for 30 minutes, or until the rice on top is tender. Fluff up with a fork and serve with plain yogurt if liked. This needs no accompaniment.

Simple chicken parcels three ways

I love roasting a whole bird, and pan-frying chicken is also good, but I can't always be bothered. So this is where the "simple" parcel-baking method comes into play, where steam inside the parcel "roasts" the chicken, keeping the meat lovely and juicy without charring. Here are three delicious citrus-perfumed recipes featuring very different marinades for you to try.

SERVES 2

2 boneless, skinless chicken breasts, about 7oz each (if using smaller ones, you will need to reduce the cooking time accordingly)

Maldon sea salt flakes and freshly ground black pepper

FENNEL & ORANGE

1 tablespoon olive oil

grated zest of 1 unwaxed orange

1 teaspoon fennel seeds

½ teaspoon garlic granules

RAS EL HANOUT & LEMON

1 tablespoon olive oil

finely grated zest of 1 unwaxed lemon

1 teaspoon ras el hanout

THYME, LIME, CUMIN & PUL BIBER

1 tablespoon olive oil

finely grated zest of 1 unwaxed lime

½ teaspoon thyme leaves

½ teaspoon ground cumin

½ teaspoon pul biber chile flakes

Preheat the oven to 425°F. Line a baking pan with parchment paper.

Tear off a sheet of parchment paper large enough to generously enclose your 2 chicken breasts to form a parcel. Place the chicken breasts on one half of the sheet, then divide the ingredients for the marinade of your choice onto them and, using your hands, coat the surface of each breast thoroughly. Season generously with salt and pepper.

Gather one edge of the parchment paper and fold over the chicken breasts to enclose them, then crimp the edges of the paper together tightly until you have a sealed parcel. Place on the lined pan and bake for 15 minutes until cooked through.

Remove from the oven and let the chicken rest in the parcel for at least 5 minutes before cutting it open and serving.

SERVE WITH /// Bazaar Spiced Chickpea & Feta Salad (see page 43) or Sweet Potato, Sage & Feta Tart (see page 150).

Yogurt & spice-fried chicken strips

In this recipe the Greek yogurt is not only a great tenderizer for the chicken but it is also a fantastic way to give the chicken an outer coating of flavor. Mayonnaise spiked with harissa and lime juice makes the perfect dipping sauce for these crispy chicken tenders.

SERVES 2 TO 4

¾lb chicken mini tenders
vegetable oil, for frying

For the marinade
⅔ cup Greek yogurt
2 teaspoons dried wild oregano
1 teaspoon paprika
1 teaspoon pul biber chile flakes
1 teaspoon garlic granules
1 teaspoon celery salt
1 teaspoon ground white pepper

For the seasoned flour
1¼ cups all-purpose flour
2 teaspoons dried wild oregano
2 teaspoons garlic granules
1 teaspoon celery salt

To serve
mayonnaise
harissa
lime wedges

Mix all the marinade ingredients together in a bowl until evenly combined. Add the chicken tenders and turn until well coated in the marinade. Cover the bowl with plastic wrap and let marinate in the refrigerator overnight or up to 24 hours. You can cook them immediately, but the marinating time will let the flavors permeate the chicken surface.

When you are ready to fry, place a skillet over medium-high heat, pour in about 1 inch of vegetable oil and bring to frying temperature. (Add a breadcrumb. If it sizzles immediately, the oil is hot enough.) Line a plate with a double layer of paper towels.

Mix the seasoned flour ingredients together in a bowl until evenly combined. One by one, shake the excess yogurt marinade from the chicken tenders, dip in the flour to coat, then back into the marinade (you won't need much) and back in the flour to coat again.

Once all the chicken pieces are dipped, add them to the hot oil and fry for 3 minutes or so on each side until nicely browned. Remove with a slotted spoon and transfer to the lined plate to drain. Add harissa and lime juice to the mayonnaise to taste, then serve alongside the chicken with extra lime wedges.

SERVE WITH /// Crushed New Potatoes with Tahini Butter & Scallions (see page 147) or Sautéed Corn with Pul Biber Honey Butter (see page 166).

Etlí güveç

My best friend Aysegül lives in Istanbul, and her family taught me everything I know about Turkish cuisine. The word *güveç* is the name of the earthenware dish in which this aromatic lamb and vegetable mixture is traditionally cooked, but a lidded casserole dish works just as well.

SERVES 4 TO 6

olive oil

1¾lb trimmed boneless lamb shoulder, cut into 1-inch cubes

2 large onions, halved and thinly sliced into half-moons

4 bay leaves

1 large head of garlic, cloves separated, peeled and kept whole

1 teaspoon dried mint

1 teaspoon dried wild oregano

1 large red bell pepper, cored, seeded, and cut into big chunks

1 large yellow bell pepper, cored, seeded, and cut into big chunks

1lb 2oz potatoes, peeled and cut into slices ½ inch thick, then halved

2 tablespoons Turkish pepper paste (optional)

¼ cup tomato paste

½ teaspoon pul biber chile flakes

1½ cups boiling water

3 to 4 slices of lemon

Maldon sea salt flakes and freshly ground black pepper

Preheat the oven to 350°F.

Pour enough olive oil into a large ovenproof casserole dish (or Dutch oven) to generously coat the bottom. Add the lamb, season well with salt and pepper, and stir to coat. Scatter with the onions, bay leaves, and garlic cloves.

Mix the mint and oregano together, then sprinkle one-third of the mixture into the dish. Using your hands, coarsely toss the onions, bay leaves, garlic, and dried herbs together without disturbing the meat. Add the peppers and potatoes and sprinkle with another third of the dried herb mixture.

Dissolve the pepper paste (if using) and tomato paste in the boiling water, add the chile flakes, and season very generously with salt and pepper (add enough seasoning for the whole dish), then pour the mixture into the casserole dish. Lay the lemon slices on top, sprinkle with the remaining dried herb mixture, and drizzle generously with olive oil.

Cover the contents of the dish with a layer of parchment paper and press firmly to push everything down. Cover the pan with a lid and bake on the lowest rack of the oven for 2½ to 3 hours. This needs no accompaniment.

Sticky spiced-apple pork belly slices

Pork belly slices are readily available and require much less fuss than a whole pork belly. This is my twist on the classic roast pork with apple sauce but packing in a lot more flavor and giving every bite a sticky appeal that leaves you wanting more. It's great served with rice, or in a bun with pickled cucumbers.

SERVES 2 TO 4

1lb 10oz pork belly slices
   (about 5 slices, 5½oz each)

For the marinade
¼ cup ready-made apple sauce
2 tablespoons soft light brown sugar
1 tablespoon red or white wine
   vinegar
1 tablespoon light soy sauce
1 teaspoon garlic granules

1 teaspoon ground coriander
1 teaspoon ground cinnamon
½ teaspoon sweet smoked paprika
   (Spanish pimentón)
Maldon sea salt flakes and freshly
   ground black pepper

To serve
steamed rice
cucumber batons

Preheat the oven to 350°F. Line a baking pan with parchment paper.

Mix all the marinade ingredients together in a small bowl until well combined.

Decant half the marinade into a large mixing bowl, add the pork belly slices, and roll them over to coat them in the mixture.

Transfer the pork belly slices to the lined pan, cover with a double layer of foil, seal tightly, and then roast for 1¼ hours.

Remove from the oven and turn the oven up to 475°F. Take off the foil and spread the remaining marinade evenly onto the pork belly slices, then roast uncovered for another 15 minutes. Serve immediately with rice and cucumber batons.

SERVE WITH /// Curried Yellow Split Peas with Sweet Potatoes & Spinach (see page 164) or Fragrant Lime, Rosemary, Coconut & Black Bean Rice (see page 196).

Za'atar, paprika & garlic chicken

Quick and easy in the oven is the way forward. I love the ease of throwing a load of ingredients into a roasting pan and just popping it in the oven, especially when the results are really good and make you think you want to do this again. Happy days.

SERVES 2 TO 3

6 large bone-in, skin-on chicken thighs

2 tablespoons olive oil

1 heaped tablespoon za'atar

1 tablespoon paprika

finely grated zest of 1 unwaxed lemon
   and juice of ½

Maldon sea salt flakes and freshly ground
   black pepper

Preheat the oven to 350°F. Line a roasting pan with parchment paper.

Put the chicken thighs into a mixing bowl, drizzle with the olive oil, and add the spices, lemon zest and juice, and a generous amount of salt and pepper. Using your hands, mix until the thighs are well coated in the mixture on both sides.

Place on the lined pan and roast for 1 hour until nicely browned and cooked through (check on them after 45 minutes). Serve immediately.

SERVE WITH /// Baked Halloumi with Lemon, Wild Thyme & Honey (see page 33) or Spiced Orzo Polow (see page 204).

Golden pork stir-fry

Inspired by my love of the Thai dish *pad krapow moo*, this spicy little stir-fry is really quick to come together and great served simply on lettuce leaves. It's also delicious with rice or noodles, and a fried egg on top makes it very nearly perfect. You can use any type of ground meat, but I do love pork and it allows the spicing to turn it the color of warm summer sunshine.

SERVES 4

vegetable oil

4 fat garlic cloves, crushed

1lb 2oz ground pork

3 teaspoons ground turmeric

1 teaspoon dried red chile flakes
(or 2 long red chiles, finely
chopped, if preferred)

1 tablespoon superfine sugar

2 teaspoons fish sauce (or just salt to
taste, if preferred)

¾ to 1¼ cups fresh cilantro,
coarsely chopped

freshly ground black pepper

rice or lettuce leaves, to serve

Heat a large skillet over medium-high heat and drizzle in enough vegetable oil to lightly coat the bottom. Add the garlic and then immediately add the ground pork, turmeric, and chile flakes (or fresh chiles), working quickly to incorporate the ingredients without burning the garlic. Stir-fry the pork about 8 minutes or so until fully cooked, but don't let it burn.

Add the sugar, fish sauce (or salt), and a generous amount of pepper and mix well.

Remove the skillet from heat and stir in the cilantro. Serve immediately spooned into lettuce leaves or with rice.

SERVE WITH /// Spicy Nutty Roasted Cauliflower (see page 160) or Sticky Tamarind, Garlic & Tomato Green Beans (see page 172).

Lemon, coriander seed & chile chicken

Coriander haters, fear not! This lovely chicken recipe features the subtle earthy, lemon flavor of coriander seeds and not the punch of the leaves, which some people have an aversion to. When I first designed this dish, I was aiming for a Cantonese-style lemon chicken, but it has evolved into something different again, Sabrina style. Not only is it flavorful, it's pretty simple to throw together, and great served with rice.

SERVES 4 TO 6

1½lb boneless, skinless chicken breasts (about 4 medium breasts)

1 unwaxed lemon

3 tablespoons honey, plus extra for drizzling

1 tablespoon coriander seeds

vegetable oil

½ teaspoon dried red chile flakes, plus extra for garnish

4 fat garlic cloves, very thinly sliced

2 teaspoons butter

Maldon sea salt flakes and freshly ground black pepper

Split each chicken breast lengthwise down the middle, then thinly slice into strips. Set aside.

Using a vegetable peeler, cut strips of peel from the lemon, then very thinly slice the peel into matchsticks and set aside. Squeeze the juice from the lemon, discarding any seeds. Mix the lemon juice with the honey and set aside.

Heat a dry skillet over high heat, add the coriander seeds, and toast for 1 minute, shaking the skillet intermittently to prevent them from burning.

Transfer the toasted seeds to a mortar and lightly crush them with the pestle, just enough to break each one, then set aside.

Drizzle some vegetable oil into the skillet over high heat, add the chicken, and stir-fry for 1 minute. Add the coriander seeds, chile flakes, garlic, and lemon peel and stir-fry again for a couple of minutes. Pour in the lemon juice and honey mixture and add a generous amount of salt and pepper. Mix well to ensure the chicken is evenly coated, then add the butter and cook for a few minutes until the glaze thickens and looks glossy and the chicken is cooked through. Serve immediately drizzled with more honey and extra chile flakes.

SERVE WITH /// Lemon, Cumin & Harissa Cabbage (see page 158).

Lamb, barberry, pine nut & pul biber kofta

Looking back at all the kofta recipes I have written to date, I realize that in most I incorporate a combination of spices, aromatics, and an element of crunch to make them special. I also sometimes add dried fruit, such as currants, raisins, sour cherries, or even cranberries. But for these beauties, I've paired the very Persian barberry with pine nuts. This works so well as a stand-alone kofta piled into a baguette or tortillas with some harissa-spiked yogurt and salad, or serve with rice.

MAKES 8 KOFTA

1lb 2oz ground lamb (20% fat)

4 scallions, thinly sliced from root to tip

1 heaped tablespoon dried wild oregano

2 tablespoons dried barberries

2 teaspoons pul biber chile flakes

1 teaspoon cumin seeds

1 teaspoon ground coriander

2 garlic cloves, crushed

⅓ cup pine nuts

½ teaspoon baking soda

Maldon sea salt flakes and freshly ground black pepper

To serve (optional)

2 mini baguettes

sliced pickled cucumbers

sliced scallions

handful of pomegranate seeds

sprigs of dill

mixed salad leaves

Greek yogurt with harissa

Preheat your oven to its highest setting. Line a baking pan with parchment paper.

Put all the ingredients into a mixing bowl with a generous amount of salt and pepper and, using your hands, work them together really well for a couple of minutes until you have an evenly combined paste.

Divide the meat mixture into 8 portions (to be as precise as possible, if you have a set of kitchen scales, you can weigh the mixture and then divide it) and shape each into an even-shaped sausage about 4 inches long.

Place on the lined pan and bake for 12 to 14 minutes, depending on how hot your oven is, until browned on top.

Serve in baguettes with extra fillings of your choice, or on their own with a side dish.

SERVE WITH /// Super-Quick Smoky Tomato Couscous (see page 199) or Tangy Bulghur Wheat Bake with Roasted Onions (see page 207).

Bloody Mary spatchcocked chicken

The number of times I have made this marinade and thought it would be great with vodka over ice! And so Bloody Mary Chicken was born. Although this recipe has no vodka in it, it is a reliable marinade that I turn to time and again, and even my stepkids like it despite the fact it is a little spicy. Spatchcocking a chicken is the genius trick to halve the cooking time of a bird, and why not? That means dinner is ready in 45 minutes—the same time it takes to dial for a takeout and have it delivered. I know which I prefer!

SERVES 4 TO 6

3¼lb chicken

For the marinade
2 tablespoons garlic oil
juice of ½ lime
3 tablespoons Sriracha
2 tablespoons tomato paste
1 tablespoon curry powder
1 teaspoon garlic pepper
1 teaspoon celery salt

Preheat the oven to 425°F. Line a large baking pan with parchment paper.

To spatchcock the chicken, place it breast-side down on a cutting board. Using a pair of poultry shears or heavy-duty kitchen scissors, cut down either side of the backbone and then remove the bone. Turn the chicken over breast-side up and gently press down on it with both hands until as flat as possible. Transfer the flattened chicken to the lined baking pan.

Mix all the marinade ingredients, except for the celery salt, in a small bowl. Rub the marinade all over the chicken and allow to marinate for 15 minutes.

Season with the celery salt, then roast for 40 to 45 minutes until deeply browned and cooked through.

Remove from the oven, cover in foil, and let stand for 10 to 15 minutes before serving.

SERVE WITH /// Fennel, Feta, Orange & Pistachio Salad (see page 39) or Fenugreek & Pepper Potatoes (see page 154).

Spiced crispy pork scallops

This quick and easy take on a pork schnitzel is a great way to use an economical lean cut of pork while giving it a good injection of flavor and a lovely crunch to finish. Whether piled into a baguette or, my favorite, served with crispy french fries, lots of lemon juice squeezed over really brings out the flavors in the coating.

SERVES 4

1lb 2oz pork loin

2 tablespoons all-purpose flour

2½ cups panko or 1½ cups other
   dried white breadcrumbs

1 heaped tablespoon dried oregano

1 heaped tablespoon garlic granules

2 teaspoons paprika

1 large egg

vegetable oil

Maldon sea salt flakes and freshly
   ground black pepper

lemon wedges, to serve

Cut the pork fillet into slices ½ inch in thickness and gently beat them flat with your fist. Dust the scallops with the flour on both sides.

Mix together the breadcrumbs, oregano, garlic granules, and paprika in a bowl and season very generously with salt and pepper.

Beat the egg in a separate bowl.

Heat a skillet over medium heat, pour in about 1 inch of vegetable oil, and bring to a very low frying temperature. (Add a breadcrumb. If it bubbles without sizzling too much, the oil is hot enough.) Line a plate with a double layer of paper towels.

One by one, dip each scallop in the beaten egg and shake off the excess, then dip in the breadcrumb mixture to coat, patting the crumbs onto the scallop to help them stick on both sides.

Add the scallops to the hot oil (in batches if necessary to avoid overcrowding the skillet) and gently fry for 2 to 3 minutes on each side until golden brown and cooked through.

Remove from the skillet with a slotted spoon and transfer to the paper-lined plate to drain. Serve immediately with lemon wedges for squeezing over.

SERVE WITH /// Sautéed Corn with Pul Biber Honey Butter (see page 166) or Spice-Roasted Celeriac with Honey, Orange & Pul Biber (see page 168).

Chorizo, potato, corn, tomato & onion bake

This recipe is a combination of some of my favorite ingredients simply thrown together and baked in a roasting pan. Isn't that how some of the best recipes in the world are born? It's sweet, savory, juicy, meaty, soft, and salty all at once—a riot of flavor. Just try it.

SERVES 4

10½oz mini cooking (raw) chorizo sausages

14oz can diced tomatoes

2 potatoes, peeled and cut into ½-inch cubes

2 red onions, quartered, then cut into 1-inch chunks

about 1⅔ cups canned kernel corn, drained

1 teaspoon cumin seeds

1 teaspoon fennel seeds

1 heaped teaspoon pul biber chile flakes

Maldon sea salt flakes and freshly ground black pepper

Preheat the oven to 400°F.

Select a suitable large roasting pan or ovenproof dish. Cut the mini chorizo sausages in half lengthwise and add to the pan with all the other ingredients and a generous amount of salt and pepper. Using 2 spoons, toss everything together until well combined.

Roast for 1 hour and serve immediately. This needs no accompaniment.

Lazy one-pan souvlaki & fried potatoes

Whenever I am in Greece, one of the very first things I want to get my hands on is a fantastic souvlaki that I can pile into a wrap with the obligatory fried potatoes and a load of tzatziki for the finish. I have shared many of my favorite kebab recipes with you before, but this one has a lazy twist, as I have managed to combine both the meat and the potato part of the recipe all in a single skillet, so there is no excuse not to try this at home.

SERVES 2

14oz trimmed boneless pork shoulder, cut into 1-inch cubes

2 tablespoons Greek yogurt, plus extra to serve

finely grated zest of 1 unwaxed lemon and juice of ½

1 heaped tablespoon wild oregano

1 tablespoon garlic granules

2 tablespoons garlic or olive oil

vegetable oil

10½oz potatoes, peeled and cut into ½-inch cubes

2 large tortillas

½ red onion, thinly sliced

1 large tomato, halved and thinly sliced

pickled chiles (optional)

your favorite chilli sauce (optional), to taste

Maldon sea salt flakes and freshly ground black pepper

Put the pork, yogurt, lemon zest and juice, oregano, garlic granules, and garlic or olive oil into a mixing bowl. Season generously with pepper and mix well, ensuring the pork is thoroughly coated in the yogurt mixture.

Place a large skillet over medium-high heat and pour in about ½ inch of vegetable oil. Line a plate with a double layer of paper towels.

Add the potatoes to the oil and cook for 10 to 12 minutes or until they begin to color on all sides and are cooked through.

Remove the potatoes from the skillet with a slotted spoon and transfer to the paper-lined plate to drain. Keep them warm in the oven at a low temperature, until you are ready to serve.

Wrap the tortillas in foil and warm them in the oven while you cook the meat.

Continued overleaf

Pour the excess oil out of the skillet and into a bowl (you can reuse this for another dish), leaving just a little drizzle in the pan, and heat for a minute before adding the pork pieces. Season the pork with salt and cook for a minute or so on each side until nicely browned, then remove from the heat.

To serve, spread Greek yogurt over the 2 tortillas to coat the entire surface. Divide the pork and some of the fried potatoes between the tortillas, top with the onion and tomato slices, your choice of chilli sauce and pickled chiles, if desired. Tuck the bottom end of each tortilla over the filling, then roll up.

Serve with the fried potatoes and enjoy. This needs no accompaniment.

Halloumi fatteh

I love marrying foods of different cultures. While halloumi is a Cypriot staple and *fatteh* is an Arab recipe, when two things are so incredibly delicious, I can't resist the urge to bring them together—crispy, salty halloumi topped with spiced ground beef and tahini yogurt. Double the quantity if you are in a sharing mood and have some toasted pitta bread on hand to bring it all together and mop up every last bite.

SERVES 4

9oz block of halloumi cheese

vegetable oil

9oz ground beef

1 teaspoon ground cumin

1 teaspoon paprika

1 teaspoon garlic granules

2 tablespoons pomegranate molasses

handful of pomegranate seeds

handful of chopped fresh cilantro

Maldon sea salt flakes and freshly
   ground black pepper

pitta bread, to serve

For the tahini yogurt

⅔ cup Greek yogurt

2 tablespoons tahini

1 garlic clove, minced

juice of ½ lemon

Cut the block of halloumi in half lengthwise so you have two long rectangular pieces. Cut each piece into 4 equal fingers, then cut each finger into 3 equal chunks.

Heat a skillet over medium-high heat and drizzle in a little vegetable oil. Add the ground beef and immediately break it up as finely as you can to prevent it from cooking in clumps, adding the spices and garlic granules as you do so. Season generously with salt and pepper and cook until the meat is well browned, then set aside.

Heat another skillet over medium heat, pour in about ½ inch of vegetable oil and bring to a very low frying temperature. (Add a breadcrumb—if it bubbles nicely without sizzling too much, the oil is hot enough.) Line a plate with a double layer of paper towels.

Add the halloumi to the hot oil and fry until a deep golden brown on all sides.

Continued overleaf

Meanwhile, place a small saucepan over very low heat, add the tahini yogurt ingredients with a generous amount of salt and pepper, and stir until well combined. If necessary, add some lukewarm water to thin it down to the consistency of thick heavy cream. Warm through, then remove from the heat.

Once the halloumi is cooked, remove from the pan with a slotted spoon and transfer to the paper-lined plate to drain.

To serve, arrange the halloumi on the plate first, then top with the ground beef, followed by the tahini yogurt, pomegranate molasses and seeds, and the cilantro. Serve immediately with toasted pitta bread. This needs no accompaniment.

Meatball & mushroom stroganoff

Who doesn't love a stroganoff? Even in Iran, due to our close proximity to Russia, we enjoy a good stroganoff. "Always with thin, matchstick fries," says my mother, as she recounts her memories from her youth in Tehran. I've had some really good stroganoffs in my time, from a fantastic one in St. Petersburg served with mashed potatoes, to versions with noodles, and the British interpretation with rice. Each recipe differed wildly and came in various shades from brown and beige to neon orange. This is a simplified version of the classic, and I've used meatballs just because they work really well and taste fantastic in the mushroom sauce, making it very nearly as good as the traditional beef steak, served with french fries.

SERVES 4

1lb 2oz ground beef

9oz cremino mushrooms, quartered

vegetable, olive or garlic oil

1 large onion, finely chopped

1 tablespoon paprika

1 heaped teaspoon garlic granules

1¼ cups light cream

Maldon sea salt flakes and freshly ground pepper

small handful of finely chopped chives, to garnish (optional)

french fries, mashed potatoes, or buttered tagliatelle, to serve

Roll the ground beef into approximately ¾-inch balls, to make approximately 30 to 32 mini meatballs.

Heat a dry skillet over high heat and, once hot, add the mushrooms and stir-fry without any oil until all their liquid has been released and evaporated.

Once the skillet is dry again, drizzle in a couple of tablespoons of oil, add the onion, and cook until softened and translucent. Add the meatballs, then gently shake the pan to avoid breaking or crushing them. Add the paprika, garlic granules, and a generous amount of salt and pepper, then pour the cream over the meatballs. Cook, without stirring, for a minute, then very gently stir to mix the spices evenly into the sauce.

Reduce the heat, cover the pan with a lid, and cook over low to medium heat for 10 to 15 minutes, gently shaking the lidded pan occasionally to prevent the meatballs from sticking to the bottom.

Adjust the seasoning to taste and scatter with the chopped chives (if using). Serve with crispy french fries, mashed potatoes, or buttered tagliatelle. This needs no accompaniment.

Fast & slow souk-spiced leg of lamb

Slow-roasting is one of my favorite cooking methods for lamb. All you really need to do is rifle through your kitchen cupboard, find a few ingredients to add a layer of flavor (fast), then pop it into a moderate oven and let that do the work (slowly). The results are always spectacular, and because it's slow-cooked, the meat is really tender and juicy. This is a real winner all round, as it involves very little effort for a very big reward. It's fantastic sliced and piled in warmed pitta bread with scallions, pomegranate molasses, pomegranate seeds, and a little yogurt, but also wonderful served as a roast with traditional accompaniments.

SERVES 4 TO 6

4½lb (or more) bone-in leg of lamb

For the marinade
⅔ cup Greek yogurt
2 heaped tablespoons tomato paste
4 fat garlic cloves, crushed
1 tablespoon olive oil
1 teaspoon ground cumin
1 teaspoon ground cinnamon
1 teaspoon paprika

1 teaspoon ground turmeric
1 teaspoon cayenne pepper
Maldon sea salt flakes

To serve (optional)
toasted pitta breads
sliced scallions
pomegranate seeds
pomegranate molasses
Greek yogurt

Preheat the oven to 350°F. Line a large roasting pan with parchment paper.

Mix all the marinade ingredients together in a small bowl until evenly combined. Coat the lamb all over in the marinade, then season well with salt. Place on the lined pan and roast for 1½ hours.

Remove from the oven, cover the lamb with a double layer of foil, and roast for a further 2½ hours.

Remove from the oven and let rest, still covered with the foil, for 20 to 30 minutes.

Serve in toasted pitta breads with sliced scallions, pomegranate seeds, and drizzled with pomegranate molasses and Greek yogurt.

SERVE WITH /// Bazaar Spiced Chickpea & Feta Salad (see page 43), or Jeweled Tomato Salad (see page 53), or Spice-Roasted Celeriac with Honey, Orange & Pul Biber (see page 168).

Speedy lamb shawarma

I do love a kebab. Admittedly, this is not the world's best-kept secret, as over the years I have written many kebab recipes using every kind of meat. This is my go-to when I want good value and quick, easy results. Lamb neck is completely underrated, especially for quick cooking, although it is equally good for slow-cooked dishes. (You can also use lamb shoulder or breast.) Once you try this recipe, I know it will become as firm a favorite of yours as it is mine. Serve in wraps or warmed pitta bread with yogurt, sliced onion, tomato, pickled cucumber, and cilantro leaves, or on a bed of mixed leaves with pomegranate seeds and a good drizzle of pomegranate molasses.

SERVES 2 TO 4

vegetable or olive oil

1lb 2oz lamb neck, trimmed
   of any thick top layer of fat

3½ tablespoons butter

1 teaspoon garlic granules

1 teaspoon ground cumin

1 teaspoon ground coriander

½ teaspoon cayenne pepper (or dried
   red chile flakes if you prefer)

Maldon sea salt flakes and freshly
   ground black pepper

To serve (optional)

tortillas

Greek or plain yogurt

thinly sliced red onion

sliced tomatoes

sliced pickled cucumbers

cilantro leaves

Heat a skillet over high heat and, once hot, rub some oil onto both sides of the lamb neck pieces. Place in the hot pan and sear on each side for a minute, just to seal (there is no need to cook the meat through).

Transfer the lamb to a cutting board and, using a sharp knife, cut it into wafer-thin slices as best you can. Don't worry about getting whole slices, just do what you can to make them nice and thin.

Return the lamb slices to the skillet with the butter, garlic granules, spices, and a generous amount of salt and pepper. Stir-fry over high heat for a couple of minutes until the meat is cooked but still lovely and tender, then remove from the skillet.

Serve the lamb piled into wraps with the fillings of your choice. This needs no accompaniment.

Kofta, orzo & tomato bake *with feta*

This is hands down one of my favorite bakes. It has a deeply rich tomato flavor and I love how light orzo pasta is. This dish really is an all-in-one job that requires very little effort after the prep work is done. And the best part of it? Kids adore it, so it's the ideal dish to place in the center of the table and share with family. If you happen to have any leftovers, simply add a little boiling water to refresh the sauce and reheat on the stove or in the oven.

SERVES 4 TO 6

1lb 2oz ground lamb

2¼ cups orzo pasta

1 large onion, finely chopped

1 large red bell pepper, cored, seeded, and finely diced

4 fat garlic cloves, thinly sliced

1 small pack (about 1oz) of flat-leaf parsley, finely chopped

3 tablespoons rose harissa

1 tablespoon superfine sugar

3 cups tomato puree

1¼ cups cold water

3 tablespoons olive oil

7oz feta cheese, cut into approximately ½-inch cubes

Maldon sea salt flakes and freshly ground black pepper

Preheat the oven to 400°F.

Roll the ground lamb into approximately 1-inch balls, to make about 20 to 22 mini kofta (to be as precise as possible, if you have kitchen scales, you can weigh the mixture and then divide it).

Put all the other ingredients, except the feta, into a large roasting pan, add a generous amount of salt and pepper, and stir well until evenly combined. Add the kofta and gently roll to coat them in the sauce, then scatter with the feta.

Roast for 45 to 60 minutes, or until the orzo is cooked.

Stir, then serve immediately. This needs no accompaniment.

Pomegranate chicken wings

If truth be told, this recipe has been years in the making because I have made so many versions of it but never come up with a formula that struck the right balance—until now. Pomegranate molasses can be an unruly beast and needs to be counterbalanced with other flavors, or its sharpness can be overpowering rather than pleasing. Well, I'm glad to say these little beauties are finger-licking good and I'm very happy to share the recipe with you at long last.

SERVES 4

2¼lb chicken wings

For the marinade
⅓ cup pomegranate molasses
2 tablespoons light soy sauce
2 tablespoons superfine sugar
1½oz piece of fresh ginger root,
    peeled and very finely grated
2 fat garlic cloves, crushed

Preheat the oven to 350°F. Line your largest roasting pan with parchment paper.

Mix all the marinade ingredients together in a large mixing bowl. Add the chicken wings and roll them over until well coated in the marinade.

Shake off any excess marinade, reserving it for later, lay the wings skin-side up on the lined pan, and roast for 25 minutes.

Remove from the oven and baste the wings generously with the remaining marinade, then roast for another 40 minutes until well browned and cooked through. Serve immediately.

SERVE WITH /// Spiced Lima Bean Patties (see page 136) or Fenugreek & Pepper Potatoes (see page 154).

Sloppy Sabs

This dish is a cross between an Indian keema pav and an American sloppy joe—both being a spiced ground-meat mixture with a consistency like gravy smooshed into a bun. I mean, what's not to like? I've let the curry powder take care of the flavoring so that the recipe remains nice and simple and takes just minutes to make. This is basic comfort food, and a little addition of Cheddar and chopped onion really does it for me.

MAKES ENOUGH FOR 4 TO 6 BUNS

vegetable oil

1 large onion, halved and thinly sliced into half-moons

1lb 2oz ground beef (20% fat)

1 tablespoon curry powder

1 teaspoon garlic granules

½ teaspoon cayenne pepper

2 tablespoons beef gravy mix

1 tablespoon all-purpose flour

Maldon sea salt flakes and freshly black pepper

To serve

4 to 6 brioche, burger, or hot dog buns

¾ cup grated sharp Cheddar cheese

1 small red onion, finely chopped

Heat a large skillet over medium-high heat and drizzle in some vegetable oil. Add the onion and fry until soft and nicely browned.

Add the ground beef and immediately break it up as finely as you can to prevent it from cooking in clumps. While still uncooked, add the curry powder, garlic granules, and cayenne and stir to coat the meat well.

Stir in the gravy mix and flour before adding enough boiling water to just cover the meat. Cook, stirring, for a few minutes until thickened and the meat has cooked through, then check the liquid volume and adjust the seasoning (if required).

Split the buns and toast them in a nonstick ridged grill pan over high heat or under a hot broiler for a couple of minutes.

To serve, divide the meat mixture between your buns, then top with the Cheddar and chopped onion. This needs no accompaniment.

Aab goosht

Is it a soup or a stew? I still can't decide, but to Persians this is comfort in a bowl. *Aab goosht* is a one-pot recipe. If you want to serve it the authentic Persian way, there are two traditions to observe. The first is *tee-leet*, where you tear up some Persian *lavaash* flatbread, add it to the dish to soak up the broth, then eat the stew and bread together. The second is *goosht koobideh*, meaning "pounded meat," where you remove a portion of the cooked dish and pound it into a paste using a big pestle, then eat it sandwiched between flatbreads with some sliced raw onions alongside a bowl of the remaining *aab goosht*. This dish tastes even better the next day, and also freezes well.

SERVES 4 TO 6

vegetable oil

1 large onion, coarsely chopped

4 to 6 garlic cloves, peeled and lightly bashed but kept whole

4 large tomatoes, quartered

4 dried limes (or use preserved lemons or the juice of ½ lemon)

⅓ cup tomato paste

1 teaspoon ground turmeric

3 lamb shanks

3 large potatoes, peeled and halved

14oz can chickpeas, drained

14oz can cannellini beans (or any other beans you might have), drained

Maldon sea salt flakes and freshly ground black pepper

flatbread or crusty bread, to serve

Place a large saucepan over medium heat and pour in enough vegetable oil to coat the bottom. Add the onion and cook until softened and translucent. Now add the garlic cloves, tomatoes, dried limes, tomato paste, turmeric, and a generous amount of salt and pepper and stir until combined.

Add the lamb shanks and pour over enough boiling water to cover the contents of the pan. Cover with a lid, reduce the heat a little, and simmer for 3 hours, stirring occasionally to ensure it isn't sticking to the bottom.

Using a wooden spoon gently squeeze some of the dried limes (or all if you like it sour!) against the side of the pan to release their flavor, then taste the broth and adjust the seasoning if desired.

Stir in the potatoes, chickpeas, and beans. Check the liquid volume (there should always be plenty of broth in the pan, so top off with water as necessary), and cook uncovered for another 30 minutes or so until the potatoes are cooked. Serve with plenty of flatbread or crusty bread. This needs no accompaniment.

Lamb & eggplant kebabs

My two favorite ingredients are combined in this twist on a charcoal-grilled classic. Just ensure your eggplant is properly cooked and soft to the touch. I like to serve these kebabs on flatbread or tortillas so they absorb the juices of the fatty lamb and eggplant for an added treat.

SERVES 2 TO 4

2 small to medium eggplants

1lb 2oz ground lamb (20% fat)

½ teaspoon baking soda

4 scallions, thinly sliced from root
   to tip

1 small pack (about 1oz) of dill,
   finely chopped

¼ cup tomato paste

1 tablespoon garlic granules

1 teaspoon ground turmeric

2 tablespoons olive oil

Maldon sea salt flakes and freshly
   ground black pepper

To serve

flatbreads

parsley leaves

sliced red onion

pul biber chile flakes

Preheat the oven to 400°F.

Keeping the eggplants whole, stalk included, make 4 evenly spaced horizontal cuts in each one without cutting all the way through to ensure they stay intact. Lay the eggplants in a roasting pan.

Put all the other ingredients, except the oil, into a mixing bowl with a generous amount of salt and pepper and, using your hands, work them together for a couple of minutes until you have an evenly combined paste.

Divide the meat mixture into 8 equal portions, roll each into a ball and flatten gently.

Brush the exposed flesh of the eggplants with the olive oil, then place a portion of meat mixture in between each cut until both eggplants are filled.

Push a wooden or thin metal skewer (at least 10½ inches long) through the center of each eggplant, from stalk to base, to hold everything in place, then roast for 30 minutes.

Remove from the oven and, using a pastry brush, baste the eggplants with the pan juices. Turn them over and roast for another 20 minutes until the eggplant flesh is soft. Serve immediately with flatbreads, parsley, sliced red onion, and chile flakes.

SERVE WITH /// Baked Halloumi with Lemon, Wild Thyme & Honey (see page 33) or Three Simple Ways With Rice (see page 192).

Lamb chops with yogurt & fenugreek

Lamb is my favorite meat, and chops are my favorite cut. (I can happily consume a platter of these by myself!) With the choice of every kind of seasoning, from the exotic to basic salt and pepper, this particular marinade is one I turn to regularly at home for both indoor grilling and barbecues. If you don't have time to make any accompaniments, this is a perfect dish for devouring on its own.

MAKES 8

8 trimmed lamb chops

Maldon sea salt flakes

For the marinade

⅓ cup Greek yogurt, plus extra
   to serve

1 small pack (about 1oz)
   of fresh cilantro

3 fat garlic cloves, peeled

1 teaspoon cumin seeds

1 teaspoon coriander seeds

½ teaspoon dried red chile flakes

2 heaped tablespoons dried fenugreek
   leaves

finely grated zest of 1 unwaxed lemon
   and juice of ½

2 tablespoons olive oil

generous amount of Maldon sea salt
   flakes and freshly ground black
   pepper

Put all the marinade ingredients into a blender and blitz until evenly combined and smooth.

Place the lamb chops in a wide, shallow nonreactive dish, add the marinade, and roll the chops over until well coated in the mixture. Cover the dish with plastic wrap and let marinate in the refrigerator for 1 hour, or overnight if preferred.

Remove the chops from the refrigerator at least 30 minutes before cooking to allow them to come to room temperature.

Preheat a nonstick ridged grill pan or skillet over the highest heat possible. Once super-hot, shake any excess marinade from the chops, sprinkle a little salt on one side, and place salt-side down on the pan. Cook for 2 to 3 minutes on each side, depending on thickness, until nicely charred. If you need to cook them in batches, keep one batch warm under a layer of aluminum foil while you cook the rest.

Remove from the pan and let stand on a plate for 5 minutes or so before serving with a bowl of Greek yogurt seasoned with black pepper.

SERVE WITH /// Fig, Beet, Goat Cheese, Red Chile & Walnut Salad (see page 48) or Sautéed Zucchini with Mint (see page 143).

Lamb, date & chile stew

Lamb stews are such a great and simple go-to for many of us, but I wanted to create something with a little more depth. The dates work like magic here, almost melting into the sauce to give the stew a deep richness and sweetness, while the chile flakes provide just the right kick to round it all off and give a pleasing finish to every bite. This dish tastes even better the next day and freezes beautifully. Serve with couscous, rice, flatbread, or even boiled potatoes. I also like mashing it up slightly and wrapping it inside a naan or pitta bread with some red onions.

SERVES 4 TO 6

vegetable oil

1 large onion, coarsely chopped

1¾lb boneless lamb shoulder, cut into ½-inch cubes

2 teaspoons ground cinnamon

1 heaped teaspoon cumin seeds

1 teaspoon dried red chile flakes (or ½ teaspoon if you're less brave)

4 to 6 garlic cloves, peeled and lightly bashed but kept whole

9oz best-quality dates (I use Medjool), pitted and roughly chopped

3 tablespoons red wine vinegar

Maldon sea salt flakes and freshly ground black pepper

couscous to serve (optional)

Place a Dutch oven (or large saucepan) over medium-high heat and pour in just enough vegetable oil to coat the bottom. Add the onion and cook until softened and translucent. Add the lamb and spices and stir well to coat the lamb in them, then season generously with salt and pepper.

Add the garlic cloves and cook for 5 minutes, or until softened. Now stir in the dates, followed by the vinegar. Cook for 5 minutes or so, stirring regularly.

Pour over enough boiling water to generously cover everything. Cover with a lid, reduce the heat, and simmer for 2 hours, stirring occasionally to ensure it isn't sticking to the bottom.

Check the liquid volume, topping off with water as necessary, and check and adjust the seasoning to taste. Cook uncovered for another hour or so until the meat is beautifully tender. Serve with couscous if liked.

SERVE WITH /// Spiced Orzo Polow (see page 204) or Yogurt, Marjoram & Pul Biber Flatbreads (see page 209).

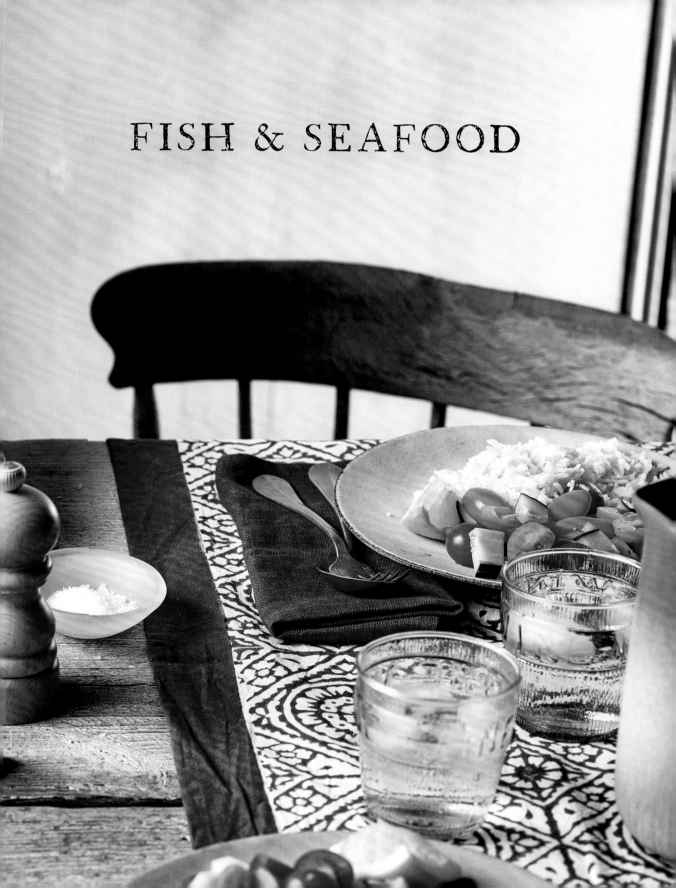

FISH & SEAFOOD

Aromatic shrimp with rice & corn

The roots of this dish come from a restaurant I used to work in where the head chef used to make a Japanese-style risotto using sushi rice, infusing ginger and other aromatics into the stock and serving it with seared scallops. I loved the dish so much that I developed a version with shrimp that I often make at home.

SERVES 2

olive oil

2-inch piece of fresh ginger root, peeled and thinly sliced into matchsticks, plus extra to serve

2 lemongrass stalks, tough 2 to 3 outer layers discarded, soft insides bashed and finely chopped

2 fat garlic cloves, minced

⅓ cup unsalted butter

⅔ cup risotto rice

2 cobs of corn, kernels sliced off

½ small pack (about ½oz) of fresh cilantro, stalks and leaves separated, both very finely chopped

about 4 cups boiling water

12 to 14 raw peeled jumbo shrimp

4 scallions, thinly sliced from root to tip, plus extra to serve

Maldon sea salt flakes and freshly ground pepper

2 pinches of pul biber chile flakes, to serve (optional)

Heat a large saucepan over medium-high heat and, once hot, drizzle in a little olive oil, add the ginger, lemongrass, and garlic and stir-fry for a minute. Add half the butter and allow it to melt while stirring the ingredients. Don't let any of the ingredients, including the butter, take on any color—remove the pan from heat if they begin to show signs of browning.

Add the rice and stir to coat in the butter mixture, followed by the chopped cilantro stalks. Add the corn and stir well, and season generously with salt and pepper.

Add a scant cup of the boiling water at a time and allow each addition to be mostly absorbed before adding the next, stirring regularly until the rice becomes creamy. (You might not need all the water.)

Add the remaining butter and keep stirring until you reach your desired consistency, then add the shrimp and cook for a couple of minutes or until they turn pink (the cooking time will depend on the size of the shrimp). Taste and adjust the seasoning if required. Finally, stir in the scallions and chopped cilantro leaves. Serve immediately, garnished with extra ginger and scallions, and sprinkled with pul biber, if you like. This needs no accompaniment.

Fragrant roasted haddock

I often feel that the delicate nature of fish means that many people forget how wonderful it is when paired with spice. Roasting whole fish on the bone is fantastic, but what about those times when you only have loins or fillets and want to avoid frying? I always turn to yogurt as a great base for creating a marinade. Not only is it a tenderizer of meats, has a flavor of its own, and creates a delicious external coating for both meats and fish, it also provides protection against high heat, allowing you to get a decent charring on the outside while keeping the flesh juicy and cooked to perfection on the inside. I have used haddock, but any firm-fleshed white fish works.

SERVES 2

¼ cup thick Greek yogurt

1 teaspoon ras el hanout

1 teaspoon ground turmeric

generous squeeze of lemon juice

about 1 tablespoon garlic or olive oil

10½oz haddock loin, cut into
   1½-inch chunks

Maldon sea salt flakes and freshly
   ground black pepper

Preheat your oven to its highest setting. Line a roasting pan with parchment paper.

Mix all the ingredients, except for the fish, together in a small bowl, and season generously with salt and pepper.

Coat the pieces of fish in the marinade, place in the lined pan, and roast for 8 to 10 minutes (depending on how hot your oven is) until just cooked through. Serve immediately.

SERVE WITH /// Braised Celery with Black Pepper & Garlic (see page 138) or Broccoli with Ginger, Lime, Garlic & Tomato (see page 141).

Sesame & spice roasted salmon

This is a Ghayour house go-to classic—I always have the spice mix sitting ready blended in a jar waiting to be put into action. Its formula was inspired by the Japanese seasoning shichimi togarashi. I ran out of it on one occasion when roasting salmon and was forced to come up with an alternative seasoning of my own, and so this spice mix was born. The method of cooking salmon in this recipe is easy and foolproof. You don't even need oil, as salmon is fatty by nature, so expect this dish to become a staple. Leftovers are great at room temperature for lunchboxes the next day, and also perfect for flaking and adding to salads and cooked grains.

SERVES 2 TO 4

4 salmon fillets, about 4½oz each

Maldon sea salt flakes

For the spice mix

1 teaspoon garlic granules

1 teaspoon paprika

1 teaspoon cayenne pepper

1 teaspoon sumac

2 teaspoons sesame seeds

generous amount of freshly ground
   black pepper

lemon wedges, to serve

Preheat the oven to 425°F. Line a roasting pan with parchment paper.

Combine all the spice mix ingredients in a small bowl. Rub the mixture all over the flesh of the salmon fillets, then season well with salt.

Place the salmon in the lined pan and roast for 10 to 12 minutes (depending on how hot your oven is).

Serve immediately with nice big wedges of lemon for squeezing over.

SERVE WITH /// Georgian Kidney Bean Salad (see page 50) or Sweet Potato, Sage & Feta Tart (see page 150).

Tomato & tamarind shrimp *with fenugreek*

I do think shrimp is somewhat underutilized in stews and saucier dishes, as we tend to favor broiling or frying them. This is a lovely dish that hits many comforting notes for me. A sweet and sharp tomato base with juicy shrimp is just the ticket when you want something a bit different, and it is great accompanied with rice but is equally delicious when mopped up with good bread.

SERVES 2

3 tablespoons olive oil

4 fat garlic cloves, thinly sliced

1 heaped tablespoon dried
    fenugreek leaves

1 tablespoon harissa

14oz can diced tomatoes

1 tablespoon unsweetened
    tamarind paste

1 tablespoon superfine sugar

8 raw colossal shrimp (or 12 to 16
    raw jumbo shrimp), shell on or off

Maldon sea salt flakes and freshly
    ground black pepper

basmati rice or crusty bread, to serve

Place a saucepan over medium heat and drizzle in the olive oil. Add the garlic and cook until translucent. Then add the fenugreek and harissa and stir well.

Pour in the tomatoes and add the tamarind and sugar, followed by a generous amount of salt and pepper, and stir well. Reduce the heat and simmer the sauce, stirring occasionally, for about 20 minutes until slightly reduced.

Add the shrimp and roll them over to coat them in the sauce, then cover the pan with a lid and cook them for 2 to 3 minutes until opaque and cooked through (larger shrimp may need a longer cooking time).

Serve with basmati rice or crusty bread.

SERVE WITH /// Fragrant Lime, Rosemary, Coconut & Black Bean Rice (see page 196) or Lemon, Cumin & Harissa Cabbage (see page 158).

Spicy orange & harissa-glazed cod

A stroke of accidental genius led to this recipe being created. I was cooking for an elderly neighbor of mine, who is a pescatarian and loves bold flavors and spices, and I turned to my kitchen cupboards to dig out some harissa and then found an orange knocking around. The flavor is incredible and reminds me of my childhood exploits in the USA, gorging myself silly on the orange chicken popular in some Chinese restaurants at that time. It is such a bold combination that just shouldn't work with fish, but it really does, and creates a kind of savory caramel coating that protects the delicate flesh while giving it an outstanding flavor on the outside.

SERVES 2

vegetable oil

2 chunky skinless cod fillets, about
    5½oz each

2 tablespoons honey

1 tablespoon rose harissa

finely grated zest of 1 unwaxed small
    orange and juice of ½

Maldon sea salt flakes and freshly
    ground black pepper

Heat a skillet over high heat and, once hot, drizzle in a little vegetable oil. Season the cod fillets on both sides with pepper, place in the skillet, and let them cook for 2 to 3 minutes on each side *without* moving them around the pan. Then season on both sides with salt.

Mix the honey, harissa, and orange zest and juice together in a small bowl until well combined, then pour over the cod. The mixture should bubble ferociously in the skillet and become thick and sticky. Using a spoon, baste the fish with the mixture and, as it thickens, it will coat the fish to glaze it evenly. Serve immediately.

SERVE WITH /// Three Simple Ways with Rice (see page 192) or Freestyle Stuffed Tomato Dolma (see page 163).

Marmalade shrimp
with barberry, chile & chive butter

I've realized that thinking outside the box when cooking is sometimes necessary to keep things fresh and avoid a cycle of repetition. Increasingly, I find myself turning to my kitchen cupboard for inspiration from more unusual suspects. For example, jams, ketchups, vinegars, and chutneys have all provided me with flavor bases for various recipes, and I've added jams, honey, and marmalade to many marinades. So this combination isn't really surprising, and the lovely, sticky sauce complements the sourness of the barberries perfectly.

SERVES 2 TO 4

¼ cup unsalted butter, at room temperature

1 tablespoon finely chopped dried barberries

¼ cup very thinly sliced or snipped chives

2 heaped tablespoons marmalade

½ teaspoon dried red chile flakes

olive oil

9oz raw peeled jumbo shrimp

Maldon sea salt flakes and freshly ground
   black pepper

crusty bread, to serve

Put the butter, barberries, chives, marmalade, chile flakes, and a generous amount of salt and pepper in a small bowl and beat together until evenly combined.

Heat a skillet over high heat and, once super-hot, drizzle in a little olive oil, add the shrimp, and stir-fry for 1 minute until they are slightly browned around the edges.

Remove the skillet from heat, add the butter mixture to the shrimp, and stir to coat. Serve immediately with crusty bread.

SERVE WITH /// Freestyle Stuffed Tomato Dolma (see page 163).

Za'atar sea bass

Considering how easy it is to make, this feels like a pretty refined and sophisticated dish, mostly because the fillets look so beautiful when coated with the za'atar, but also because sea bass always feels a bit fancy and special. Either way, it takes a few minutes to make and tastes sensational.

SERVES 2

1 heaped tablespoon za'atar

1 tablespoon all-purpose flour

vegetable oil, for frying

2 skin-on sea bass fillets, about
    3½oz each

Maldon sea salt flakes and freshly
    ground black pepper

lemon wedges, to serve

Mix the za'atar, flour, and a generous amount of salt and pepper together in a wide, shallow dish, such as a pasta bowl.

Dredge both sides of the sea bass in the seasoned flour to coat (if the fish is bone dry, wet the surface a little with water so that the flour sticks).

Place a skillet over medium-high heat and drizzle in enough oil to coat the bottom. Once hot, add the sea bass fillets to the pan, skin-side down, and cook for 1 to 2 minutes until the skin is crisp. Turn the fillet over and cook for another minute until the flesh is just cooked. Serve immediately, crispy skin-side up, with a lemon wedge for squeezing over.

SERVE WITH /// Broccoli with Ginger, Lime, Garlic & Tomato (see page 141) or Braised Celery with Black Pepper & Garlic (see page 138).

Pan-fried spiced shrimp

Shrimp is such a convenience food for me. When I manage to find colossal or super colossal shrimp, of which you need only two or three per person, they are pretty spectacular with a simple spice coating. I can't resist tandoori shrimp. They're one of my all-time favorite ways to enjoy these giant shellfish, so this is my little nod to that spectacular dish.

SERVES 2

6 super colossal raw shrimp (ideally about 8 to 12 shrimp per pound but you can use a larger quantity of smaller shrimp), peeled but tails left on

vegetable oil

½ lemon, to serve (optional)

For the marinade

⅓ cup Greek yogurt

2 teaspoons curry powder

1 teaspoon ground turmeric

generous squeeze of lime juice

very generous amount of Maldon sea salt flakes and freshly ground black pepper

Mix all the marinade ingredients together in a mixing bowl. Add the shrimp and roll them over until well coated in the marinade.

Heat a large skillet over high heat and, once hot, drizzle in a little vegetable oil. Add the shrimp and cook for a couple of minutes or so on each side until opaque and firm to the touch (smaller shrimp will need a shorter cooking time).

Halve the lemon, add it to the pan, and fry the flesh sides. Serve the shrimp immediately with the fried lemon quarters for squeezing over.

SERVE WITH /// Spicy Nutty Roasted Cauliflower (see page 160) or Three Simple Ways with Rice (see page 192).

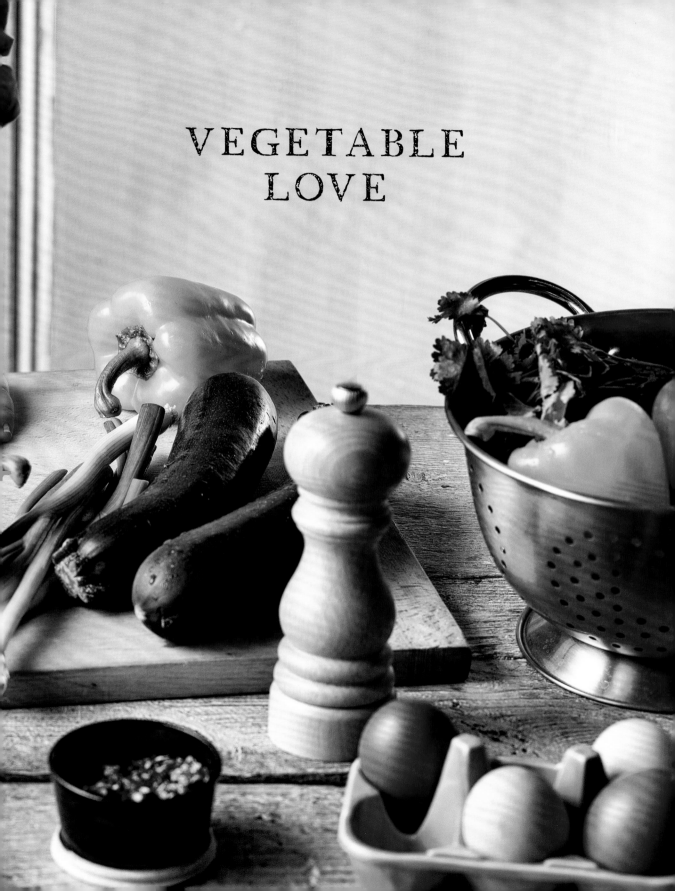

VEGETABLE LOVE

Ash-e-Reshteh

Classed as a soup of sorts by Persians, this is rich and packed full of herbs and legumes, along with noodles called *reshteh*, meaning "strands." These can be tricky to find, so I tend to use spaghetti. *Kashk* (or whey) is the traditional accompaniment, but if you can't find it, use labneh or Greek yogurt.

SERVES 6 TO 8

olive oil

2 large onions, finely chopped

3 tablespoons dried fenugreek leaves

1 teaspoon ground turmeric

2¼ cups chopped fresh cilantro

2 cups chopped flat-leaf parsley

9oz baby spinach leaves

2 tablespoons all-purpose flour

14oz can chickpeas

14oz can green lentils

14oz can kidney beans

14oz can borlotti or cannellini beans

3½oz spaghetti

Maldon sea salt flakes and freshly ground black pepper

To serve

store-bought crispy fried onions

kashk (whey), labneh or Greek yogurt (optional)

2 tablespoons dried mint

2 tablespoons olive oil

Heat a very large saucepan over medium-high heat and, once hot, drizzle in some oil, add the onions, and stir-fry until translucent and beginning to turn golden around the edges. Stir in the fenugreek and turmeric with the cilantro and parsley and cook until the fresh herbs are completely wilted, without any browning (they need to lose their vibrant green color and look like well-cooked spinach). Add the spinach leaves and a generous amount of salt and cook for 10 to 15 minutes until the spinach is well cooked and has reduced.

Add the flour and stir thoroughly to avoid clumping, then add a very generous amount of salt and pepper and all the legumes and their brine. Pour in enough boiling water to cover the contents of the pan, reduce the heat, and simmer for 45 minutes, stirring *very* carefully now and then (so as not to break down the legumes) and keeping an eye on the liquid volume to ensure that it doesn't dry out or stick to the bottom. If it looks like the water is evaporating too quickly, reduce the heat or cover the pan with a lid to preserve the liquid, but bear in mind that you want it to be thick and hearty rather than watery.

Check the seasoning and adjust accordingly, then add the spaghetti, stir gently, and cook for 10 minutes. Stir again and cook for another 30 minutes.

Meanwhile, place a small saucepan over medium heat, add the dried mint and olive oil and heat the mint for a few minutes, without letting it burn. Remove the pan from the heat.

To serve, scatter with the crispy fried onions and add a spoonful of whey, labneh, or yogurt if you wish. Finally, drizzle the mint oil over the top. This needs no accompaniment.

Pomegranate-glazed eggplant
with peanuts & scallions

I love eggplant, and the easier the cooking method, the better the recipe. So here is a nice and easy way to roast them, with a deliciously sharp yet sweet glaze and a flourish of extras to finish the dish. Life needn't be complicated and the simple things are often the best.

SERVES 2 TO 4

2 large eggplants, peeled and cut into
   round, 1-inch thick slices

3 to 4 tablespoons olive oil

2 tablespoons pomegranate molasses

3 tablespoons honey or maple syrup

1 scallion, thinly sliced diagonally from
   root to tip

generous handful of salted peanuts,
   toasted and coarsely chopped

Maldon sea salt flakes

Preheat the oven to 425°F. Line a large roasting pan with parchment paper.

Brush both sides of the eggplant slices with the olive oil, arrange in a single layer in the lined pan, and roast for 22 to 25 minutes until cooked through but not browned.

Mix the pomegranate molasses and honey together until evenly combined. Use a pastry brush to brush the mixture evenly over the eggplant on both sides, then sprinkle with a little salt. Roast for another 5 to 6 minutes until the glaze is thick and sticky.

Scatter with the chopped scallion and peanuts before serving.

SERVE WITH /// Spiced Mushroom Loqmeh Lettuce Wraps with Sesame Seeds, Yogurt & Tamarind Sauce (see page 12) or Seared Pepper Steak & Tomato Salad with Sweet & Spicy Lime Dressing (see page 44).

Spiced Lima bean patties

Good things are born out of simplicity and necessity, and these patties are exactly that. Nothing could be quicker or easier to make, but they are also incredibly delicious and versatile enough to be packed into wraps or buns with the addition of some grated cheese, or served with a fried egg on top. And you can make mini ones if you so wish.

MAKES 4

14oz can Lima beans, drained

1 tablespoon all-purpose flour, plus extra for dusting

1 garlic clove, crushed

1 teaspoon pul biber chile flakes

½ teaspoon ground cumin

½ teaspoon paprika

½ teaspoon ground turmeric

1 tablespoon apricot jam

vegetable oil, for frying

generous handful of natural or dried white breadcrumbs

Maldon sea salt flakes and freshly ground black pepper

To serve (optional)

chutney or mango sauce

tortillas

finely sliced scallions

cilantro leaves

lime wedges

Put all the ingredients, except the breadcrumbs and oil, into a mini food processor with a generous amount of pepper and blitz together until smooth. You can also mash the ingredients together in a bowl using a masher or the end of a rolling pin, if need be.

Heat a large skillet over medium-high heat and pour in enough vegetable oil to coat the bottom.

Meanwhile, shape the bean mixture into 4 patties. Dust both sides of each patty with a little flour, then press into the breadcrumbs to coat.

Fry the patties gently for 3 to 4 minutes on each side until a deep golden brown.

Season with salt and serve immediately with chutney or mango sauce, in tortillas with sliced scallions, cilantro leaves, and with lime wedges for squeezing over.

SERVE WITH /// Spiced Mushroom Loqmeh Lettuce Wraps with Sesame Seeds, Yogurt & Tamarind Sauce (see page 12) or Pomegranate Chicken Wings (see page 101).

Braised celery *with black pepper & garlic*

I can hear you celery haters turning the page of this recipe as I write, but I defy you not to fall in love with it. Braised celery is so underrated, and the cooking method means it loses some of the characteristics that many seem to dislike to leave a wonderfully tender texture and deliciously delicate flavor. Social media can be endlessly inspiring, so when I spotted a simple braised celery dish on chef Milli Taylor's Instagram feed when I had some celery lying around, I quickly threw this recipe together. And guess what? It was pretty spectacular considering its glorious simplicity. I served it with some leftover rice, and I immediately knew I had to share the recipe with you. Try adding chicken, beef, or lamb strips right at the end, and quick-cooking them in the same pan, then serve with steamed basmati rice.

SERVES 4 TO 6

vegetable oil

1 bunch of celery, stalks separated and cut into ½-inch wide, 2-inch long pieces

1 heaped teaspoon coarsely ground black pepper

1 large head of garlic, cloves separated and thinly sliced

1 tablespoon rice wine vinegar

1½ cups good-quality chicken or vegetable or vegan stock

Maldon sea salt flakes

steamed rice, to serve

Place a large saucepan over high heat. Drizzle in some vegetable oil, add the celery, and stir-fry for 2 minutes. Add the pepper and garlic and stir-fry for another 2 minutes without allowing the celery to brown too much but enabling it to soften as much as possible.

Stir in the vinegar, then add the stock and let the liquid bubble and cook for 10 to 15 minutes, stirring occasionally to prevent the celery from burning but allowing any excess liquid to reduce down.

Reduce the heat and continue cooking the celery until it loses its crunch and turns limp. Serve with rice or stirred into noodles.

SERVE WITH /// Fragrant Roasted Haddock (see page 117) or Za'atar Sea Bass (see page 127).

Broccoli with ginger, lime, garlic & tomato

I absolutely love broccoli, it is so pleasingly versatile. But sometimes you want to add a little more pep to your broccoli, and in using up some past-their-best tomatoes and a few other bits to make this stir-fried dish, I realized I was onto a good thing. Hand on heart, I ate almost the entire dish straight from the pan, and have made it many times since because it's just so good. Don't try to preserve the bright green color of the broccoli, unless you want crunchy florets. Instead, focus on flavor and ensure the broccoli is cooked to your liking. This is also great stirred into noodles or pasta, or served with steamed basmati rice.

SERVES 4

1 tablespoon vegetable or olive oil

1oz fresh ginger root, peeled and very finely grated

3 fat garlic cloves, finely chopped

1lb broccoli florets (if using a whole head of broccoli, thinly slice the stalk using a vegetable peeler and add to the florets)

4 to 5 large tomatoes (or use cherry or baby tomatoes), chopped

½ cup boiling water

2 tablespoons superfine or granulated sugar

finely grated zest and juice of 1 unwaxed lime

Maldon sea salt flakes and freshly ground black pepper

Place a large skillet or saucepan over medium-high heat. Drizzle in the oil, add the ginger and garlic, and stir-fry for a minute.

Wash the broccoli and add it to the pan without shaking off the excess water, then quickly stir to coat it in the garlic and ginger mixture before adding the tomatoes.

Pour the boiling water into a large measuring cup, stir in the sugar until dissolved, then add the lime juice. Pour the mixture into the pan, stirring as you go. Season generously with salt and pepper, cover the pan with a lid, and cook for 5 minutes.

Stir again, replace the lid, and cook for another 2 to 3 minutes until the sauce has somewhat reduced and thickened and the broccoli is tender to the bite. Check and adjust the seasoning to taste, then stir in the lime zest and serve.

SERVE WITH /// Fragrant Roasted Haddock (see page 117) or Za'atar Sea Bass (see page 127).

Sautéed zucchini *with mint*

When I first tried this dish I really didn't expect to enjoy it because the idea of zucchini with vinegar didn't appeal to me, but oh how wrong I was. Fried zucchini slices in olive oil with fresh mint and vinegar…how could something so simple be so wonderful? Well, it just is. Try it! You won't look back.

SERVES 4 TO 6

3 to 4 tablespoons olive oil

2 large zucchini, very thinly sliced

1 tablespoon vegan red or
   white wine vinegar

5 sprigs of mint, leaves
   coarsely chopped

Maldon sea salt flakes and freshly
   ground black pepper

Heat a large skillet over medium-high heat and, once hot, add the olive oil followed by the zucchini slices and fry until they begin to brown around the edges.

Season with salt and also a very generous amount of pepper, about double what you would usually use, then toss the zucchini in the seasoning. Add the vinegar, which will sizzle, and toss the zucchini again as best you can.

Continue cooking the zucchini for a few minutes until soft and nicely browned, then add the mint, toss the zucchini once more, and serve.

SERVE WITH /// Lamb Chops with Yogurt & Fenugreek (see page 109).

Cheat's dhal

I can't tell you how much I love dhal of every description. I grew up eating one variation or another, despite it not being remotely Persian, and to this very day it's inconceivable that I could eat an Indian meal in a restaurant without ordering it. For me, no dhal can come close to dhal makhani—a labor of love, cooked slowly with a heavy spice blend and a huge amount of butter and cream, thus not for the faint-hearted. One day my desire for said dhal became unbearable and I wondered if I could recreate a similar richness in a fraction of the time with ready-cooked lentils. Well, this is, of course, completely different from dhal makhani – but I confess that the satisfaction levels are every bit as high, especially when you have some rice, naan, or good bread to eat it with. It also makes for a very indulgent baked-potato filling, to which I like to add a little chopped raw onion and grated Cheddar for the ultimate treat.

SERVES 4 TO 6

2 to 3 tablespoons vegetable oil

1 large onion, finely chopped

1 teaspoon ground cumin

1 teaspoon ground turmeric

1 teaspoon ground coriander

½ teaspoon ground cinnamon

½ teaspoon dried red chile flakes

3 tablespoons tomato paste

2 x 14oz cans green lentils, drained

¼ cup butter

⅔ cup heavy cream

1¼ cups boiling water

Maldon sea salt flakes and freshly
  ground black pepper

Heat a saucepan over medium-high heat and, once hot, drizzle in the vegetable oil, add the onion, and stir-fry until translucent and beginning to turn golden around the edges.

Add all the spices and stir well to coat the onion as best you can, then add the tomato paste and stir again until evenly combined, and cook for 2 minutes. Stir in the lentils, then add the butter, allow it to melt, and stir it in. Pour in the cream, season very generously with salt and pepper, stir well, then pour in the boiling water and stir again.

Reduce the heat and simmer gently for 30 minutes, stirring occasionally, until the dhal is thick, rich, and creamy. Check and adjust the seasoning to taste, stir and serve with bread or plain rice.

Crushed new potatoes with tahini butter
& scallions

Tahini butter is one of my more indulgent recent experiments. New potatoes are firm and delicious, and the ideal vehicle to carry the nutty flavor of the tahini butter. The perfect accompaniment to many a dish, a little goes a long way with these beauties, but they are ever so satisfying and the pepper provides a lovely kick to the overall flavor of the butter.

SERVES 4 TO 6

1lb 10oz new potatoes

½ cup butter

⅓ cup tahini

1 bunch of scallions, thinly
  sliced from root to tip

pul biber chile flakes, for sprinkling

Maldon sea salt flakes and freshly
  ground black pepper

Cook the new potatoes in a saucepan of boiling water for 20 to 25 minutes (depending on size) until cooked through and tender.

Drain the potatoes and return to the pan, then add the butter, tahini, and a generous amount of salt and pepper. Using a masher, lightly crush the potatoes, then switch to a wooden spoon and mix to ensure the butter and tahini are evenly combined. Finally, stir in the scallions.

Serve with a sprinkle of pul biber to finish.

SERVE WITH /// Yogurt & Spice-Fried Chicken Strips (see page 67).

Cumin & lemon asparagus

When asparagus is in season I tend to gorge myself senseless until I've eaten half my body weight of the stuff. Then I can rest easy, knowing that when the season comes to an end I'll have had my fill. This recipe really is simplicity exemplified, and while I love my asparagus bathed in butter for the most part, adding a little twist on the classic is always a treat, too.

SERVES 4

1 teaspoon cumin seeds

vegetable or olive oil

9oz asparagus spears
  (snap off the woody ends)

¼ cup unsalted butter

finely grated zest of 1 unwaxed lemon
  and juice of ½

Maldon sea salt flakes and freshly
  ground black pepper

Heat a dry skillet over medium heat, add the cumin seeds, and toast for 1 to 2 minutes, or until they release their aroma, shaking the pan intermittently to prevent them from burning.

Drizzle a little oil into the pan, add the asparagus, and roll them over to coat them in the seeds. Add a good tablespoon of cold water and shake the pan before adding the butter and a generous seasoning of salt and pepper. Cover the pan with a lid and cook for about 5 minutes or so until tender, shaking the pan occasionally with the lid still on (thicker asparagus may need a little longer).

Once cooked, add the lemon zest and juice and toss the asparagus to combine evenly, then serve.

SERVE WITH /// Halloumi, Bacon, Date & Apple Salad (see page 31) or Seared Pepper Steak & Tomato Salad with Sweet & Spicy Lime Dressing (see page 44).

Sweet potato, sage & feta tart

This quick, easy, and delicious recipe is a real lifesaver for a midweek supper when you lack inspiration but have store-bought pastry on hand. Perfect as a brunch or lunch dish, too.

SERVES 4 TO 6

1 x 11oz ready-rolled puff pastry sheet

olive oil

9oz sweet potato, peeled and very thinly sliced

7oz feta cheese

1 long red chile, seeded and thinly sliced

½ small pack (about ½oz) of sage,
　leaves picked

honey, for drizzling

Maldon sea salt flakes and freshly ground
　black pepper

Preheat the oven to 400°F.

Place the pastry sheet, on the parchment paper it comes with, on a baking sheet. Score a border about ½inch wide around the edges of the pastry and brush olive oil all over the pastry within the border.

Place the sweet potato slices in a mixing bowl, add a good drizzle of olive oil, and season generously with salt and pepper. Using your hands, give them a mix to ensure the slices are all lightly coated in oil but not overly greasy.

Arrange the slices, slightly overlapping, on the pastry sheet within the border. Season well with salt and pepper and drizzle with a little more oil. Crumble the feta evenly over the top, scatter with the chile slices, and dot the sage leaves on top. Bake for 25 to 30 minutes until nicely browned.

Remove from the oven, drizzle with honey, and serve.

SERVE WITH /// Three Ways with Chicken (see page 64) or Sesame & Spice-Roasted Salmon (see page 119).

Pomegranate & harissa-roasted eggplant

This recipe was born out of having an eggplant left over from recipe testing and trying to make myself a quick lunch. It was so delicious and looked so beautiful that I had to share it with you. I have since made it many times, and every time I serve it, the response is almost always, "That's an eggplant? It looks like a steak!"

SERVES 4

2 large eggplants

3 tablespoons garlic oil

2 tablespoons rose harissa

2 tablespoons pomegranate molasses

2 tablespoons honey

Maldon sea salt flakes

Preheat the oven to 425°F. Line a roasting pan with parchment paper.

Peel the eggplants, then cut them in half lengthwise. Using a sharp knife, score criss-cross lines about ½ inch apart in the flat side of each half, cutting no deeper than ½ inch into the flesh.

Place the eggplant halves, cut-side up, on the lined pan, brush the scored surfaces very generously with the garlic oil until you have used it all up, and roast for 30 minutes.

Meanwhile, mix together the rose harissa, pomegranate molasses, honey, and a generous amount of salt in a small bowl.

Remove the eggplant halves from the oven and, using a teaspoon, spoon the harissa mixture evenly over them to coat generously, then roast for another 10 minutes. Serve immediately.

SERVE WITH /// Fast & Slow Souk-Spiced Leg of Lamb (see page 95) or Freestyle Stuffed Tomato Dolma (see page 163).

Fenugreek & pepper potatoes

Fenugreek leaves are so underrated in Western cuisine, whereas Asians and we Persians have been using them in our cooking for years. Finally, supermarkets have begun to stock them as well as fenugreek seeds and ground fenugreek. The aroma of this magical herb is so punchy that it fills the kitchen. I absolutely love it and will champion its virtues until the cows come home. Adding it to these potatoes gives them so much dimension and flavor, and the pepper provides a very pleasing kick, too.

SERVES 4

- 1 heaped tablespoon ghee or 2 tablespoons vegetable oil
- 4 large round red or round white potatoes, about 5½oz each, cut into slices ⅛ inch thick
- 2 tablespoons dried fenugreek leaves
- 1 long red chile, seeded and thinly sliced (optional)
- 1 teaspoon garlic granules
- 1 teaspoon ground coriander
- ½ teaspoon coarsely ground black pepper
- 3 tablespoons cold water
- Maldon sea salt flakes
- Greek yogurt, to serve

Heat a saucepan over medium-high heat (or medium if using a gas stove) and add the ghee or vegetable oil. Add the potatoes and then all the other ingredients, except the water, with a generous amount of salt and mix well to coat the potatoes evenly in the herbs and seasonings. Cook for 6 to 8 minutes, stirring occasionally, until the potatoes start to brown.

Add the cold water and stir once more, then cover with a lid and cook for about 15 to 20 minutes, swirling the pan a few times (hold the lid down firmly) to prevent the ingredients from burning or sticking to the bottom.

Stir before serving with some Greek yogurt.

SERVE WITH /// Bloody Mary Spatchcocked Chicken (see page 80) or Pomegranate Chicken Wings (see page 101).

Golden pepper, cheese & zucchini kuku

Persians have a fundamental love for all things *kuku*, which is the Persian equivalent of a frittata. Since I have already covered the classic *kuku* recipes in my previous books, I would like to share this new invention with you. I just love bell peppers and cheese cooked with eggs—they make a fantastic partnership—and this sunny-colored frittata is great served hot or cold as a main course, side dish, or brunch dish. You can of course use cheeses other than Cheddar, such as feta, goat cheese, or your favorite grated hard cheese. I like to cut the frittata into slices and serve it either on its own, with a salad, or piled into flatbread or wraps with a nice tangy, spicy sauce, such as a sweet tamarind ketchup.

SERVES 4 TO 6

6 eggs

2 tablespoons Greek yogurt

1 bunch of scallions, thinly sliced
   from root to tip

1 red bell pepper, cored, seeded,
   and finely diced

1 yellow bell pepper, cored, seeded,
   and finely diced

1 zucchini, coarsely grated

5½oz sharp Cheddar cheese

1 tablespoon ground turmeric

1 heaped teaspoon garlic granules

1 tablespoon all-purpose flour

1 teaspoon baking powder

1 small pack (about 1oz) of fresh
   cilantro or flat-leaf parsley,
   finely chopped

Maldon sea salt flakes and freshly
   ground black pepper

Preheat the oven to 400°F. Line an 8-inch square cake pan with parchment paper.

Beat the eggs in a mixing bowl, then add all the other ingredients and mix together with a fork until evenly combined. Be careful not to overbeat as the mixture will become stiff.

Pour the mixture into the lined pan, then use the fork to even out the filling and give the pan a gentle shake to settle the ingredients. Bake for 25 minutes until lightly browned on top and a knife inserted comes out clean. Allow to cool slightly before serving.

SERVE WITH /// My Ultimate Tuna Salad (see page 15) or Ottoman Puffs (see page 20).

Lemon, cumin & harissa cabbage

Cabbage is one of my great loves, but this really is next-level cabbage flavor. While the spicing here is bold, the sweetness of the cabbage still comes through and works really well with the spice without remotely overpowering it. To make this dish vegan, substitute maple syrup or superfine sugar for the honey, and either omit the butter or use a plant-based alternative spread.

SERVES 4 TO 6

1 heaped teaspoon cumin seeds

1 head of pointed cabbage,
    halved, cored, and cut into
    slices ½ inch thick

olive oil

2 tablespoons cold water

1 tablespoon rose harissa

1 heaped tablespoon honey

finely grated zest of 1 unwaxed lemon
    and a generous squeeze of ½

2 tablespoons butter

Maldon sea salt flakes and freshly
    ground black pepper

Place a dry saucepan over medium heat, add the cumin seeds, and toast them for 1 to 2 minutes, or until they release their aroma, shaking the pan intermittently to prevent them from burning.

Add the cabbage and stir to coat it in the cumin seeds, then drizzle in a little olive oil (less than a tablespoon) and quickly sauté, adding the cold water to also steam the leaves. You can turn the heat up slightly, but be careful not to brown or burn the cabbage.

Add the rose harissa, honey, and lemon juice, then stir well to coat the cabbage evenly in the sauce. Season to taste with salt and pepper, add the butter, and cook for 2 minutes, stirring, to allow it to melt into the sauce.

Finally, add the lemon zest and serve immediately.

SERVE WITH /// Lemon, Coriander Seed & Chile Chicken (see page 76) or Tomato & Tamarind Shrimp with Fenugreek (see page 120).

Spicy nutty roasted cauliflower

Cauliflower has to be one of my all-time favorite vegetables (along with broccoli and cabbage). Give it to me in soups, stews, and even raw as a crudité and I can't get enough. Roasting cauliflower has become hugely popular, but I wanted a satay-inspired flavor here and I am very happy with the results. Try it and see just how flavorful it is. And don't forget to scrape off all the bits of sauce that have stuck to the pan and add them to your plate. They are delicious!

SERVES 4 TO 6

1 large cauliflower, cut into florets

For the marinade

14oz can coconut milk

3 heaped tablespoons smooth peanut butter

1 tablespoon superfine sugar

1 teaspoon ground turmeric

1 teaspoon garlic granules

½ teaspoon cayenne pepper

To serve

Greek yogurt

cilantro leaves

handful of roasted peanuts

freshly ground black pepper

Preheat the oven to 350°F. Line your largest roasting pan with parchment paper.

Put all the marinade ingredients into a large mixing bowl and, using a whisk, gently beat together until evenly combined and smooth. Add the cauliflower florets and, using your hands, roll them gently in the mixture until they are evenly coated.

Place the florets on the lined pan, pouring any excess marinade over the flowering end of the florets. Roast for 45 minutes until tender and just starting to turn brown.

Spread a layer of Greek yogurt onto a serving platter, then arrange the cooked cauliflower on top. Scrape all the remaining bits of sauce onto the cauliflower, then sprinkle with the cilantro leaves and the peanuts, and grind over some black pepper before serving.

SERVE WITH /// Lamb Chops with Yogurt & Fenugreek (see page 109) or Pan-Fried Spiced Shrimp (see page 129).

Freestyle stuffed tomato dolmas

Why don't we stuff vegetables more? Every time I make stuffed bell peppers or dolmas of any kind, I always wonder why I don't do it more often. Stuffing is the perfect vehicle for using up odds and ends. I've called these "freestyle" tomatoes because while I've given you a basic recipe, I wholeheartedly encourage you to switch up the herbs and ingredients and use whatever you like. Add feta, chiles, nuts, and other chopped up vegetables or leftover meat—the choice is yours! Dolmas are a humble gem of an idea that deliver big in return. These can be made and cooked the day before to allow the flavors to develop—simply eat cold or reheat.

MAKES 2

- 2 very large beefsteak tomatoes
- 2 tablespoons basmati rice
- 8 pitted green or black olives, coarsely chopped
- 2 teaspoons non-pareil (small) capers in brine
- handful of chopped fresh oregano leaves (or 1 teaspoon dried oregano)
- handful of chopped flat-leaf parsley
- 2 scallions, thinly sliced from root to tip
- 1 tablespoon tomato paste
- 1 teaspoon garlic granules
- Maldon sea salt flakes and freshly ground black pepper

Preheat the oven to 425°F. Select an ovenproof pan or dish that the tomatoes will fit in.

Carefully cut the top off each tomato, retaining it as a lid. Using a teaspoon, carefully scoop out all the insides, being careful to avoid tearing the tomato skin. Pour any juice into a mixing bowl, then finely chop the flesh and add to the bowl.

Add all the other ingredients to the mixing bowl along with a little salt and a generous amount of pepper and combine well. Check and adjust the seasoning if desired. Remember that you need to add enough to season the rice, so be generous.

Set the scooped-out tomatoes in your ovenproof dish and divide the rice mixture between them, leaving space at the top for the rice to expand. Cover with their lids and bake for 30 minutes.

Remove from the oven, cover the dish with foil, then bake for a further 45 minutes.

SERVE WITH /// Spicy Orange & Harissa Glazed Pan-Fried Cod (see page 122), or Marmalade Shrimp with Barberry, Chile & Chive Butter (see page 124), or Pomegranate & Harissa-Roasted Eggplant (see page 153).

Curried yellow split peas
with sweet potatoes & spinach

Many people just don't know what to do with yellow split peas, but they are incredibly versatile and economical. They work especially well with herbs and spices, such as garlic, ginger, and chile. I use them to make meatballs, fritters, and a version of falafel, as well as stews, like this one, which is fabulous with bread or rice, or served as a soup if you thin it down with water.

SERVES 4 TO 6

1 teaspoon black mustard seeds

1 teaspoon fennel seeds

2 tablespoons olive oil

1 large onion, finely chopped

1 cup yellow split peas, soaked overnight, then drained

¼ cup unsalted butter

2 tablespoons curry powder

2½ cups cold water

9oz sweet potatoes, peeled and cut into ½-inch cubes

3¼ cups baby spinach leaves

Maldon sea salt flakes and freshly ground black pepper

crusty bread, such as a baguette, to serve

Heat an empty saucepan over medium-high heat, add the mustard and fennel seeds, and toast for 1 minute, shaking the pan intermittently to prevent them from burning.

Drizzle in the olive oil, add the onion, and stir-fry until translucent and beginning to turn golden around the edges.

Add the split peas, then the butter, curry powder, and a generous amount of salt and pepper and stir-fry for 2 minutes.

Pour in the cold water and stir once more. Reduce the heat, cover the pan with a lid, and simmer gently for 30 to 35 minutes, stirring occasionally.

Stir in the sweet potato cubes (and more water if the pan is getting dry), then cook, uncovered, for a further 20 to 25 minutes until the sweet potatoes are cooked through.

Remove the pan from the heat, add the spinach, and stir through. Replace the lid and let stand for 5 minutes, then give everything a final stir before serving with crusty bread.

SERVE WITH /// Yogurt, Marjoram & Pul Biber Flatbreads (see page 209) or Sticky Spiced-Apple Pork Belly Slices (see page 70).

Sautéed corn *with pul biber honey butter*

I can eat corn all day long. Ever since I was a kid, I would open a can of kernel corn and just eat spoonfuls of it on its own. I'd like to tell you that I have grown out of this habit, but the truth is that on occasions when I am making something that uses canned kernel corn, several spoonfuls never make it as far as the recipe because I can't resist indulging! However, there is no better corn than fresh corn, either enjoyed on the cob, or sliced off and bathed in butter, as here,. This simple, spicy-yet-sweet, flavored butter served with fresh kernels is perfection.

SERVES 2

1 tablespoon olive oil

2 cobs of corn, kernels sliced off

1 heaped teaspoon dried wild oregano

¼ cup unsalted butter

1 heaped tablespoon honey

1 teaspoon pul biber chile flakes

Maldon sea salt flakes and freshly
   ground black pepper

Heat a skillet over medium heat and, once hot, drizzle in the olive oil. Add the corn and cook for a few minutes, stirring occasionally.

Add the oregano and a generous amount of salt and pepper and stir well. Then add the butter, allow it to melt, and cook the corn for a few more minutes.

Stir in the honey until dissolved, then add the pul biber and stir again. Serve immediately.

SERVE WITH /// Yogurt & Spice-Fried Chicken Strips (see page 67) or Spiced Crispy Pork Scallops (see page 82).

Spice-roasted celeriac *with honey, orange & pul biber*

I love root vegetables because they stand up beautifully to spices, chile heat, and bold flavors and really do deserve to be used more. Still so budget-friendly yet seriously underrated, celeriac is a particular favorite of mine, as it's quite different from its sweeter counterparts (such as parsnips and carrots) and has a mellow acidity that holds sweet and spicy flavors especially well. Simply roasted here with a sticky glaze, I promise you I could casually eat half a pan of it before it even gets to the plate. This is great topped with a little goat cheese or pile both together in a wrap.

SERVES 4 TO 6

about 2¼lb celeriac, peeled and
   cut into chunks approximately
   1 inch thick
about 3 tablespoons garlic or olive oil
2 teaspoons cumin seeds
2 teaspoons coriander seeds
Maldon sea salt flakes and freshly
   ground black pepper

For the glaze
3 tablespoons honey
finely grated zest and juice of
   1 unwaxed orange
2 teaspoons pul biber chile flakes
   (reserve 2 pinches for sprinkling)

Preheat the oven to 425°F. Line your largest roasting pan with parchment paper.

Place the celeriac chunks in the lined pan and drizzle generously with the oil. Add the cumin and coriander seeds and a generous amount of salt and pepper, then rub the oil and spices all over the celeriac until evenly coated.

Spread the celeriac out into a single layer and roast for 30 minutes until the edges are nicely browned.

Meanwhile, mix the glaze ingredients together in a small bowl until evenly combined.

Remove the celeriac from the oven, drizzle with the glaze, and roll the chunks over in the mixture until well coated, then roast for another 10 minutes.

Remove from the oven, give the celeriac a final toss in the sticky glaze, then transfer to a wide platter. Sprinkle with the reserved pul biber, and serve.

SERVE WITH /// Spiced Crispy Pork Scallops (see page 82) or Fast & Slow Souk-Spiced Leg of Lamb (see page 95).

Sweet potato & halloumi stuffed röstis

Fried potatoes in any incarnation are always a joy. Röstis have long been a love of mine, but these, with a halloumi stuffing, are a little different—a perfect pairing with the sweet and crunchy sweet potato exterior.

MAKES 4

½lb sweet potatoes, peeled

3 scallions, thinly sliced from
  root to tip

1 teaspoon ground cumin

1 teaspoon pul biber chile flakes,
  plus extra to serve

1 teaspoon dried wild oregano

1 tablespoon all-purpose flour

1 egg, beaten

vegetable oil, for frying

4½oz halloumi cheese, coarsely grated

Maldon sea salt flakes and freshly
  ground black pepper

To serve

Greek yogurt

arugula leaves

Grate the sweet potato on the coarse side of a box grater. Using a double layer of paper towels, pat as much excess moisture as possible out of the sweet potato to ensure it is nice and dry.

Put the grated sweet potato into a mixing bowl with the scallions, spices, oregano, flour, egg, and a generous amount of pepper and, using a fork, mix together lightly until just combined (don't overwork the mixture). Divide into approximately 4 equal portions and set aside.

Heat a skillet over medium-high heat, pour in ½inch of vegetable oil, and bring to frying temperature. (Add a pinch of the mixture. If it sizzles immediately, the oil is hot enough.) Line a plate with a double layer of paper towels.

Shape the sweet potato portions into patties, as flat as possible. Place one-quarter of the halloumi in the center of each patty and wrap the sweet potato mixture around it as best you can.

Place the röstis in the hot oil, pat them flat with a spatula, and fry for 4 minutes or so on each side until nicely browned and crispy all over.

Remove from the pan with the spatula, transfer to the paper-lined plate, and pat dry. Season with salt, then serve with Greek yogurt sprinkled with a little extra pul biber, and an arugula salad.

SERVE WITH /// Fragrant Roasted Haddock (see page 117) or Sesame & Spice-Roasted Salmon (see page 119).

Tahini & thyme mushrooms

Mushrooms and thyme are a great match for each other, but tahini really works here, too. It's a simple enough recipe with a nod to garlicky mushrooms in cream sauce, but with the creaminess coming from tahini instead of the usual heavy cream or crème fraîche. Delicious served on top of some toasted sourdough bread.

SERVES 2 TO 4

14oz cremino mushrooms, quartered

olive oil

1 tablespoon garlic granules

1 teaspoon dried wild thyme

3 tablespoons tahini

½ cup lukewarm water

½ small pack (about ½oz) of flat-leaf parsley, coarsely chopped

Maldon sea salt flakes and freshly ground black pepper

toasted sourdough, to serve

Heat a large, dry skillet over high heat and, once hot, add the mushrooms and stir-fry without any oil until all their liquid has been released and evaporated.

Once the pan is dry again, drizzle in a little olive oil, add the garlic granules, wild thyme, tahini, and a generous amount of salt and pepper and stir until evenly combined.

Add the lukewarm water and mix well, then add the chopped parsley and stir again before serving on toasted sourdough.

SERVE WITH /// Three Ways with Chicken (see page 64) or Za'atar, Paprika & Garlic Chicken (see page 72).

Sticky spiced harissa & lime roasted carrots
with feta & barberries

Roasted carrots have long been a favorite of mine, but these are really next level and yet still ridiculously simple to throw together. They also provide more proof that there aren't many things that a sticky glaze won't improve. It will definitely ensure the whole pan gets eaten up and you won't be stuck with any leftovers.

SERVES 6 TO 8

2 ¼lb carrots, peeled and cut diagonally ½-inch thick slices

about 3 tablespoons garlic or olive oil

1 teaspoon coriander seeds

1 teaspoon black mustard seeds

3½oz feta cheese

½ pack (about ½oz) of fresh cilantro, finely chopped

generous handful of flaked almonds

2 tablespoons dried barberries

Maldon sea salt flakes and freshly ground black pepper

For the glaze

2 heaped tablespoons honey

2 tablespoons harissa

finely grated zest and juice of 2 unwaxed limes

Preheat the oven to 425°F. Line your largest roasting pan with parchment paper.

Place the carrot slices on the lined pan, drizzle generously with the oil, enough to coat all of them, and rub all over the carrots. Add the coriander seeds and mustard seeds and roll the carrots over to coat them.

Spread the carrots out into a single layer, season generously with salt and pepper, and roast for 30 minutes.

Meanwhile, mix the glaze ingredients together in a small bowl until evenly combined.

Remove the carrots from the oven, drizzle with the glaze, and roll the carrots in it until well coated. Then roast for another 10 to 12 minutes until nice and sticky.

Remove from the oven, give the carrots a final toss in the glaze, then transfer to a wide platter.

Crumble the feta evenly over the carrots, then sprinkle with the chopped cilantro. Scatter with the flaked almonds and the barberries and serve.

SERVE WITH /// Bloody Mary Spatchcocked Chicken (see page 80) or Fragrant Roasted Haddock (see page 117).

Broccolini with tahini garlic sauce
& preserved lemon

Quick, delicious, easy to make, and eaten in minutes. That's what you hope all vegetable dishes turn out to be, and I usually find that when something is so easy to put together, I end up making it more often. This is particularly good because it can be eaten on its own, but you can also add pasta or grains to it for a more substantial dish.

SERVES 4

7oz broccolini

1 heaped tablespoon tahini

2 to 3 tablespoons lukewarm water

2 preserved lemons, finely chopped

1 fat garlic clove, minced

2 tablespoons olive oil

freshly ground black pepper

Bring a saucepan of water to a boil, add the broccolini, and cook for 5 to 6 minutes.

Meanwhile, mix the tahini with the lukewarm water in a small bowl to loosen it to a saucelike consistency. Add the preserved lemons, garlic, and a generous amount of pepper and mix well.

Drain the broccolini and tip into a bowl. Drizzle with the olive oil, then pour in the sauce and stir until the broccolini is well coated. Serve immediately.

SERVE WITH /// Three Ways with Chicken (see page 64) or Spicy Orange & Harissa Glazed Pan-Fried Cod (see page 122).

Za'atar, leek, potato & Gruyère frittata

While I have called this a frittata, the addition of heavy cream makes it seem more like a quiche. Leek and potatoes are a classic combination, and I've added a little Gruyère because cheese and potatoes are a match made in heaven. But it's the fragrant addition of za'atar that makes this unique and totally delicious. Hot or cold, it's a real winner.

SERVES 4 TO 6

olive oil

14oz potatoes, peeled and cut into small cubes (less than ½ inch)

14oz leeks, cut into slices ¼ inch thick, tough ends trimmed and discarded

1 heaped teaspoon garlic granules

2 tablespoons za'atar

¾ cup coarsely grated Gruyère cheese

½ cup heavy cream

8 eggs, beaten

Maldon sea salt flakes and freshly ground black pepper

Preheat the oven to 425°F.

Select a large ovenproof nonstick skillet and place it over medium-high heat. Once hot, pour in enough olive oil to coat the bottom. Add the potato cubes and cook until they begin to soften and brown. Add the leeks and cook for 10 minutes or so until soft and cooked through. Add the garlic granules and za'atar and stir well, then season the mixture very generously with salt and pepper, bearing in mind that you are also seasoning the eggs to come. Stir thoroughly, then reduce the heat to medium.

Add the Gruyère and cream to the beaten eggs and mix together with a fork, then pour over the potatoes and leeks, mix briefly until evenly combined, and cook gently for about 6 to 8 minutes.

Transfer the pan to the oven and cook for 8 to 10 minutes, or until the tip of a butter knife inserted into the center comes out clean. Remove from the oven and let cool slightly before serving.

SERVE WITH /// Tahini & Thyme Mushrooms (see page 176) or Ricotta, Mint & Harissa Roasted Broccoli (see page 185).

Ricotta, mint & harissa roasted broccoli

This is such a surprisingly delicious dish. Initially it began as a whole roasted head of broccoli, but I really liked the marinade and couldn't get enough of it, so I broke the head into florets to ensure they were better coated in it, which also ensured they cooked more evenly to boot. It's a simple treatment that yields spectacular results.

SERVES 2 TO 4

14oz broccoli florets

9oz ricotta cheese

2 tablespoons thick Greek yogurt

1 heaped tablespoon rose harissa

1 large garlic clove, crushed

1 heaped teaspoon dried mint

Maldon sea salt flakes and freshly ground
   black pepper

Preheat the oven to 375°F. Line a roasting pan with parchment paper.

Fill a kettle with water and put it on to boil.

Combine the ricotta, yogurt, harissa, garlic, dried mint, and a generous amount of salt and pepper in a large mixing bowl.

Once the kettle has boiled, fill a heatproof bowl with boiling water, plunge the broccoli into it, then cover with a plate or lid. Let stand for 5 to 6 minutes, then drain off all the water, shake the florets, and pat dry with a clean dish cloth to remove any remaining moisture.

Add the florets to the ricotta mixture and roll them until well coated all over. Spread out the broccoli on the lined pan and roast for 45 minutes. Serve immediately.

SERVE WITH /// Three Ways with Chicken (see page 64) or Za'atar, Leek, Potato & Gruyère Fritatta (see page 182).

CARBS OF ALL KINDS

Cheese, thyme & walnut flatbreads
with honey

These little flatbreads with melted cheese are so versatile that I almost always keep mini tortillas in the house just in case I want to make them. Inspired by the French *tarte flambée*, they are ready in minutes and you can use whatever you have lying around the kitchen to top them off. I've offered two very different options here, using Stilton or goat cheese, but you can use other cheeses if you prefer.

MAKES 2

2 mini tortilla wraps

1oz vegetarian Stilton
   or soft goat cheese

2 good pinches of dried wild thyme

handful of walnut pieces

1 tablespoon honey

Preheat your oven to its highest setting. Line a baking pan with parchment paper.

Place the tortillas on the lined tray. If using Stilton, crumble half of it onto each tortilla, leaving a clear 1-inch border around the edge. If using soft goat cheese, spread half of it onto each tortilla, leave a 1-inch clear border around the edge.

Sprinkle with the wild thyme and walnuts and bake for 4 to 5 minutes until the edges of the tortillas are browned.

Drizzle with the honey and serve immediately.

SERVE WITH /// Butternut Soup Two Ways (see page 27).

Three no-cook pasta sauces

Sometimes the thought of making a sauce that takes longer to cook than the pasta itself is just too much. These three no-cook sauces can be made quickly using a blender and are the ideal solution but, in true Sabrina style, they deviate from tradition and are in no way Italian. Instead, they are new and delicious ways to dress pasta in a hurry.

SERVES 3 TO 4

10½oz spaghetti or your favorite
  pasta shape
Parmesan cheese or a vegan
  alternative (optional)
Maldon sea salt flakes and freshly
  ground black pepper

WALNUT, SPINACH & HERB WITH ZUCCHINI

½ cup grated Parmesan cheese
⅓ cup coarsely chopped walnuts
1⅔ cups spinach leaves
1 fat garlic clove, peeled
1 small pack (about 1oz) of basil
1 small pack (about 1oz) of fresh
  cilantro
juice of ½ lime
about ⅓ cup olive oil, or more
  if needed
2 zucchini, grated

YOGURT, TARRAGON & PISTACHIO /// Vegetarian

⅔ cup unsalted pistachio nuts
1 small pack (about 1oz) of fresh
  tarragon, leaves picked
2 tablespoons olive or garlic oil
1 cup Greek yogurt

PEPPER, HARISSA & TOMATO /// Vegan

2 large red or yellow bell peppers,
  cored, seeded, and coarsely chopped
2 tablespoons rose harissa
2 large garlic cloves, peeled
1 x 6oz tub semi-dried tomatoes
  and their oil

Cook the pasta in a large pan of salted boiling water following the package directions.

Meanwhile, put all the ingredients for the sauce of your choice in a blender and blitz until smooth. Season well with salt and pepper.

Once the pasta is cooked, drain and add it to a large bowl. Pour your chosen sauce over it, toss to coat, if you wish, and serve immediately with Parmesan or a vegan cheese if liked. This needs no accompaniment.

Three simple ways with rice

Rice is a Persian staple, but cooking it the traditional way can be time-consuming and the results can vary greatly. So here is a straightforward and foolproof cooking method to ensure you get perfect rice every time, as well as some inspiring flavor combinations. You need never be scared of making rice again.

SERVES 4

1½ cups basmati rice

2 cups cold water

2 tablespoons butter, coarsely cut into cubes

Maldon sea salt flakes and freshly ground black pepper

HARISSA, LEMONGRASS & LIME LEAF

1 heaped tablespoon harissa

2 lemongrass stalks, tough 2 to 3 outer layers discarded, soft insides bashed and finely chopped

4 fresh lime leaves, rolled up tightly and thinly sliced into ribbons

1 tablespoon garlic granules

LEMON & HERB

finely grated zest and juice of 2 unwaxed lemons

3 tablespoons dried dill

3 tablespoons dried chives

1 tablespoon garlic granules

1 teaspoon ground turmeric

FENUGREEK & GINGER

thumb-sized piece of fresh ginger root, peeled and finely grated

3 tablespoons dried fenugreek leaves

1 tablespoon ground ginger

1 tablespoon garlic granules

1 teaspoon pul biber chile flakes

1 teaspoon ground cumin

½ teaspoon ground cinnamon

Put the rice and water in a saucepan, ideally nonstick. Add all the ingredients for your chosen variation and mix well. Season generously with salt and pepper, then stir in the butter.

Place over very low heat (low if using a gas stove), cover the pan with a lid, and cook without stirring for 30 minutes or until the rice on top is soft and tender. Fluff up with a fork and serve.

SERVE WITH /// Harissa & Lemon Roasted Chicken Thighs (see page 58), or Lamb & Eggplant Kebabs (see page 106), or Spicy Orange & Harissa-Glazed Pan-Fried Cod (see page 122), or Pan-Fried Spiced Shrimp (see page 129).

Spicy garlic, tomato & mascarpone penne
with Greek basil

This dish was inspired by the Penne alla Vodka at Café Papparazzi on Fulham Road, and as a teenager growing up in west London in the '90s, this was *the* place to be. Huge lines of young people desperate to get in, loud music, and dancing on tables until 2a.m.—ahhhh, my youth! Admittedly, this recipe is a little different from the original, as it's vodka-free, and the addition of pul biber chile flakes is more to my taste. The original didn't come with basil either, but I love the added punch of Greek basil. This is a quick and easy supper with more flavor than you would expect. I like to serve it with garlic bread.

SERVES 2

7oz penne pasta

2 tablespoons olive oil

4 fat garlic cloves, thinly sliced

2 tablespoons tomato paste

¾ cup mascarpone cheese

1 teaspoon pul biber chile flakes

2 handfuls of Greek basil leaves

Maldon sea salt flakes and freshly
   ground black pepper

garlic bread, to serve

Cook the penne in a large saucepan of salted boiling water following the package directions.

Meanwhile, place a skillet over medium heat and drizzle in the olive oil. Add the garlic and cook gently until softened and translucent. Then add the tomato paste, mascarpone, and most of the pul biber (save some for garnish) and stir until the mixture is smooth and evenly combined.

Once the pasta has cooked, use a slotted spoon to transfer it to the skillet, reserving some of the cooking water, and season generously with salt and pepper. Stir the pasta to coat it well with the sauce and add a little of the reserved water to loosen the mixture and give you a nice saucelike consistency. Sprinkle with the reserved pul biber and the Greek basil leaves and serve immediately. This needs no accompaniment.

Fragrant lime, rosemary, coconut & black bean rice

Think of this as my salute to Jamaican rice and peas – a dish I enjoy very much. My version uses black beans, which are easier to find than the classic gungo peas, and I find that a little lime zest really adds to the dish. It's a great accompaniment to a curry or stew and spiced meat or vegetable dishes, but equally good with roast chicken, and it also freezes well.

SERVES 4

vegetable oil

1 large onion, finely chopped

4 large garlic cloves, bashed, peeled, and thinly sliced

1½ cups basmati rice

2 tablespoons butter

handful of rosemary leaves

14oz can black beans, drained and rinsed

finely grated zest of 2 unwaxed limes and juice of 1

1¼ cups coconut milk

¾ cup cold water

Maldon sea salt flakes and freshly ground black pepper

Place a saucepan over medium-high heat and drizzle in a little vegetable oil. Add the onion and cook until softened and translucent. Then add the garlic slivers, stir well, and cook for another 10 minutes until the onion is soft.

Add the rice, butter, rosemary, and beans, and give the contents of the pan a quick but gentle stir before adding a generous amount of salt and pepper, followed by the lime zest and juice, coconut milk, and water, stirring well.

Cover the pan with a lid, reduce the heat, and cook gently for 20 minutes or so. Remove the lid and cook for another 15 minutes, or until the liquid has fully evaporated and the rice is soft and cooked through.

Gently fluff up the rice with a fork and serve.

SERVE WITH /// Sticky Spiced-Apple Pork Belly Slices (see page 70), or Za'atar, Paprika & Garlic Chicken (see page 72), or Tomato & Tamarind Shrimp with Fenugreek (see page 120).

Super-quick smoky tomato couscous

I am super-proud of this one. Couscous is a North African staple, but it's not always loved by everyone, and I fear that's mostly because many people don't know how to cook it and impart real flavor to it. While traditionally couscous is steamed, our Westernization of its preparation uses boiling water, which not only speeds up the process and makes it much easier, but also gives you just enough time to pack in a few extra flavors to bring out the best in it. This flavor combination is an explosion in the mouth and, best of all, you can eat it hot or let it cool and serve as a salad.

SERVES 4

½ cup couscous

2 tablespoons dried chives (or dried parsley, oregano, or marjoram)

2 heaped tablespoons tomato paste

1 teaspoon sweet smoked paprika (Spanish pimentón)

½ teaspoon dried red chile flakes (optional)

1 tablespoon good olive oil

⅔ cup boiling water

1 cup drained and halved semi-dried tomatoes in oil

generous squeeze of lemon juice

Maldon sea salt flakes and freshly ground black pepper

Put the couscous, chives, tomato paste, smoked paprika, chile flakes (if using), olive oil, and a generous amount of salt and pepper in a mixing bowl and, using a fork, mix the ingredients together until evenly combined.

Add the boiling water and stir quickly. Cover the bowl with plastic wrap and let stand for 5 minutes.

Remove the plastic wrap and use a fork to fluff up the couscous. Add the tomatoes and lemon juice and stir in carefully.

Serve immediately. Any cooled leftovers can be refrigerated and then used as a lunchbox salad the next day.

SERVE WITH /// Halloumi, Bacon, Date & Apple Salad (see page 31) or Lamb, Barberry, Pine Nut & Pul Biber Kofta (see page 79).

Lazy mantí

Dumplings are high on my list as one my favorite things. Strangely though, they don't exist in traditional Persian cuisine, despite us being sandwiched between countries that all have such dumplings, usually known as mantí. Was it the Ottomans or the Arabs or was it the Silk Road traders who brought dumplings to the Middle East from China? The truth is, I just don't know. What I do know is that the Turks do a pretty fantastic *mantí* dish laden with yogurt and sometimes a spicy butter, and there is nothing more comforting than a bowl of this when you are tired and hungry. Admittedly, I never make my own, but I have tried various ready-made dumplings, from Chinese and Russian to Polish and Italian and they are still pretty comforting. Store-bought tortelloni or other stuffed pasta are easiest to find, so that's what I'm using here, but you can use whatever dumplings you can find with any filling you like.

SERVES 2

10½oz pack of store-bought stuffed pasta (I use spinach and ricotta tortelloni)

¼ cup unsalted butter

1 teaspoon pul biber chile flakes

⅔ cup plain yogurt

1 scant teaspoon dried mint

Maldon sea salt flakes and freshly ground black pepper

Cook the stuffed pasta in a large saucepan of boiling water following the package directions, then drain into a sieve.

Return the pan to heat, and add the butter. When it has melted, stir in the pul biber, then remove from heat.

Season the yogurt with salt and pepper and stir, ensuring it has a pouring consistency like heavy cream (add some water to thin it down, if necessary).

Divide the pasta between bowls, pour the yogurt over each serving, then drizzle with the pul biber butter. Scatter with the dried mint and add a generous amount of pepper to finish. Serve immediately. This needs no accompaniment.

Sage butter, feta & black pepper pasta

When a method is really simple, I find I'm most likely to turn to that recipe again and again. This pasta dish is a case in point—easy, quick, and satisfying, perfect for a midweek meal. It also works well with fresh oregano instead of sage; either way, the gently infused herb butter really does make the dish.

SERVES 2

7oz pasta shells

⅓ cup unsalted butter

20 sage leaves

2½ tablespoons pine nuts, toasted

⅔ cup crumbled feta cheese

2 pinches of pul biber chile flakes
  (optional)

Maldon sea salt flakes and coarsely
  ground black pepper

Cook the pasta in a large saucepan of salted boiling water following the package directions.

A couple of minutes before the pasta is ready, place a skillet over very low heat. Add the butter and sage leaves and very gently melt the butter, stirring the leaves so that their flavor infuses the butter. Don't let the butter sizzle too aggressively.

Once the pasta is cooked, drain off most of the water and, using a slotted spoon, transfer the pasta to the skillet. Turn the heat up, toss the pasta in the butter, and season very generously with coarsely ground pepper and a little salt (not too much, as feta is salty). Add the pine nuts and toss to mix. Finally, add the feta and stir to mix well, allowing it to melt and coat the pasta.

Serve immediately, sprinkled with some extra pepper, and the pul biber if desired. This needs no accompaniment.

Spiced orzo polow

Many countries in the Middle East have a special vermicelli rice dish that is much revered. Persians sometimes serve it as part of their New Year festivities, but Arabs and Turks eat it on a more regular basis. I wanted to share that traditional recipe with you, but in my quest to test it to determine the correct quantities, I couldn't find vermicelli pasta anywhere, only rice vermicelli, which isn't the right kind. So that made me turn to the ricelike orzo pasta instead, as it's small enough for this use and more readily available in supermarkets. But if you do find vermicelli strands, by all means use them in place of the orzo.

SERVES 4 TO 6

about 2 tablespoons olive oil

1 large onion, finely chopped

4 fat garlic cloves, thinly sliced

⅓ cup orzo pasta

⅓ cup unsalted butter, plus extra to
    serve (optional)

2 cups basmati rice

1 teaspoon ground cinnamon

1 teaspoon ground cumin

3¼ cups cold water

Maldon sea salt flakes and freshly
    ground black pepper

Place a saucepan over medium heat and drizzle in the olive oil. Add the onion and cook until softened and translucent, then add the garlic and cook for another minute.

Add the orzo and butter, stir well, and toast until it turns golden brown.

Add the rice, spices, and a generous amount of salt and pepper and stir well until the orzo and rice are evenly coated in the melted butter and spices.

Pour in the cold water and stir well, then cover the pan with a lid. Cook for 30 to 35 minutes over very low heat (or low if using a gas stove), until the rice on top is cooked and tender.

Fluff up with a fork and serve, with a few extra lumps of butter if you like.

SERVE WITH /// Za'atar, Paprika & Garlic Chicken (see page 72) or Lamb Date & Chile Stew (see page 111).

Tangy bulghur wheat bake *with roasted onions*

Bulghur wheat is cheap and cheerful, quick to cook, and a little goes a long way. This is a really handy side dish for roasted meats, seafood, and fish, but also delicious on its own both hot and cold. Best of all, you just throw everything together, stir, and bake!

SERVES 3 TO 4

1 cup bulghur wheat

3 tablespoons pomegranate molasses

2 tablespoons tomato paste

1 tablespoon Sriracha

1 teaspoon garlic granules

1 tablespoon olive or garlic oil

2 cups cold water

2 large onions, halved, then each half cut
   into 3 wedges

Maldon sea salt flakes and freshly ground
   black pepper

Preheat the oven to 350°F. Select an ovenproof dish about 8 inches square.

Put all the ingredients except the onions into the dish, add a very generous amount of salt and pepper, and stir until all the seasonings have dissolved into the water.

Add the onion wedges and turn them over to coat them in the liquid, then space them out in the dish. Bake for 45 minutes.

Remove from the oven, fluff the grains with a fork, and serve.

SERVE WITH /// Lamb, Barberry, Pine Nut & Pul Biber Kofta (see page 79), or Fast & Slow Souk-Spiced Leg of Lamb (see page 95), or Lamb Chops with Yogurt & Fenugreek (see page 109).

Yogurt, marjoram & pul biber flatbreads

Need bread but don't have any? This simple flatbread recipe is the solution, and once you get the hang of it, you'll be knocking these out on a regular basis and can experiment with your own finishing touches. I like to crush a fat garlic clove and mix it into 2 tablespoons melted butter, then brush the butter all over the freshly cooked flatbreads before serving.

MAKES 4

¾ cup Greek yogurt

1⅔ cups all-purpose flour sifted with 2 teaspoons baking powder, plus extra flour for dusting

1 level teaspoon baking powder

2 teaspoons dried marjoram

1 teaspoon pul biber chile flakes

1 teaspoon garlic granules

olive oil

Maldon sea salt flakes and freshly ground black pepper

To serve (optional)

½ stick of butter

1 fat garlic clove, minced

Put all the ingredients, except the oil, into a mixing bowl with a generous amount of salt and pepper and, using a fork and a little drizzle of olive oil, bring everything together to form a dough.

Tip the dough onto a lightly floured work surface and knead gently for 1 minute.

Divide the dough into 4 equal portions (to be as precise as possible, if you have kitchen scales, you can weigh the mixture and divide it). Dust the work surface with a little extra flour, then roll each portion into a circle ¼ inch in thickness. This will ensure you get a nice pillowy flatbread; if rolled too thinly, they will be crisper and less light, although still delicious.

Place a dry, heavy skillet over medium heat and, once hot, add the first flatbread and cook for 2 minutes on each side. Don't be tempted to flatten the bread against the pan. Just allow it to rise naturally and brown on both sides. Transfer to a plate and fry the remaining flatbreads in the same way.

If liked, make a garlic butter by placing the butter and minced garlic in a small saucepan over a low heat until the butter melts. Brush the butter over the warm flatbreads to serve.

SERVE WITH /// Zesty Mackerel Paté (see page 24), or Butternut, Cardamom & Tahini Soup (see page 27), or Lamb, Date & Chile Stew (see page 111).

SOMETHING
SWEET

Rhubarb, rose & pistachio trifle pots

I love a good trifle. Some have jelly, while others have fruit compote, but the variations don't stop there these days. This recipe is very different from the classic, not only in the fruit and flavorings, but also in the thin slices of Madeira cake (a type of pound cake) I've used instead of ladyfingers for the base. Fond as I am of ladyfingers, I wasn't always able to find them. So, I turned to Madeira cake as an alternative. It holds its texture longer and can be cut to fit individual serving dishes without reducing to crumbs. Rose and pistachio is a characteristic Persian combination, but I now live in North Yorkshire, where there is an area known as the Rhubarb Triangle renowned for producing early forced rhubarb, so I've teamed the three ingredients together for a match made in heaven. You can make the pots in advance and refrigerate them, but wait until just before serving to add the pistachios to keep their color vibrant.

SERVES 4

14oz trimmed rhubarb (preferably thin stems), cut into ¾-inch pieces

¼ cup superfine sugar

1 teaspoon rosewater

1 scant cup heavy cream

1 heaped tablespoon confectioners' sugar

1 scant teaspoon vanilla extract

4 squares, about 2 inches each, of store-bought Madeira cake or pound cake to line the tumblers

1⅓ cups ready-made vanilla custard

handful of pistachio nuts, very finely chopped

Place a saucepan over medium heat, add the rhubarb, superfine sugar, and rosewater and mix well. Bring to a very gentle simmer and cook for about 10 to 15 minutes until the rhubarb is soft, stirring occasionally to ensure it doesn't burn. Remove from the heat and let cool.

Using a hand-held electric hand beater, whip the cream with the confectioners' sugar and vanilla extract in a mixing bowl until pillowy soft peaks form.

Line up 4 glass tumblers and push a square of cake into the bottom of each one.

Pour in one-quarter of the custard, then divide the rhubarb mixture between the tumblers and top with a layer of the vanilla cream. (Traditionally the fruit should sit on top of the cake base, but I prefer it this way—you can add the layers in any order you like.) Sprinkle with the chopped pistachios and serve.

Orange & dark chocolate rubble cake

I have been using this recipe for years, turning it out as muffins, a loaf cake, a round cake, and even a layer cake, but I've finally settled for a square pan because I really like cutting it into squares and snacking on little bites of it. It's light and airy, but the chocolate rubble is a masterstroke because every bite is different as the chocolate ratio changes throughout the cake. Try it! You won't be disappointed.

MAKES 12 SMALL
SQUARES OR 9
LARGER ONES

5½oz dark chocolate (70% cocoa solids)
4 eggs
1 cup superfine sugar
1 teaspoon orange extract (alcohol-free)
finely grated zest of 2 small unwaxed
  oranges

1¼ cups all-purpose flour
2 sticks unsalted butter, melted
1 teaspoon baking powder
¼ cup milk
confectioners' sugar, for dusting
  (optional)

Preheat the oven to 350°F. Cut a large square of parchment paper, crumple it up, then smooth it out and use to line an 8-inch square cake pan.

Break the chocolate into pieces, add to a small food processor, and pulse it until some is finely chopped while some is left in larger chunks. If doing by hand, chop the chocolate unevenly in the same way as best you can.

Put the eggs, superfine sugar, orange extract and orange zest and juice in a large mixing bowl and beat together until evenly combined. Add the flour, melted butter, and baking powder and mix again until smooth. Fold in the chocolate rubble and mix once again until evenly combined.

Pour the batter into the lined pan, then bake for 45 minutes or until a skewer or knife inserted into the center comes out clean.

Remove from the oven and let cool completely in the pan before cutting into 12 or 9 squares and serving with an optional dusting of confectioners' sugar.

Chewy pistachio bites

This three-ingredient wonder is simple to put together, but the results are pretty spectacular. Chewy, nutty, and delicious—and ready in a matter of minutes. There is one small problem with them, a serious factor that, no doubt, you won't thank me for. They are 100 percent addictive. If you're anything like me, you will be whipping up a second batch not long after the first. You can also use ground almonds as an alternative nut, but I definitely prefer pistachios.

MAKES 12

1 egg white

¾ cup confectioners' sugar, sifted,
   plus extra for dusting

¾ cup pistachio slivers (or whole nuts),
   very finely blitzed in a food processor

Preheat the oven to 375°F. Line your largest baking sheet with parchment paper.

Using an electric hand-held beater, whip the egg white in a mixing bowl until stiff peaks form. Add the confectioners' sugar and gently fold into the egg whites. Now add the ground pistachios and mix until evenly combined.

Using a teaspoon, dollop 12 equal portions of the mixture onto the lined baking sheet, spaced apart to allow them room to spread a little, then bake for 12 minutes.

Remove from oven, transfer to a wire rack, and let cool. Dust with confectioners' sugar before serving.

Frosted lemon almond loaf cake

This has quickly become our house favorite, and it's my youngest stepson's number one cake, with good reason. It is super delicious and therefore totally moreish, yet also incredibly simple to make. When I first started making it, a loaf would disappear within a couple of hours and I was baking three or four each week to keep up with demand. So beware: I've given you plenty of warning that this cake is highly addictive!

SERVES 6 TO 8

3 eggs

⅔ cup superfine sugar

2 teaspoons lemon extract
  (alcohol-free)

1 teaspoon almond extract
  (alcohol-free)

¾ cup all-purpose flour

1 teaspoon baking powder

½ cup ground almonds

⅔ cup unsalted butter, melted

finely grated zest of 1 unwaxed lemon
  and the juice of ½

For the frosting

juice of ½ lemon, left over from the
  cake ingredients

⅓ cup confectioners' sugar, sifted

hundreds and thousands (rainbow
  sprinkles), to decorate

Preheat the oven to 350°F. Line a 2-pound (9-inch) loaf pan with a nonstick parchment paper liner or cut a rectangle of parchment paper, crumple it up, then smooth it out and use to line the pan.

Put the eggs, superfine sugar, and lemon and almond extracts into a mixing bowl and beat together until well combined. Add the flour, baking powder, ground almonds, melted butter, lemon zest, and the juice of half the lemon and mix thoroughly until you have a smooth batter.

Pour the batter into the lined pan and bake for 1 hour, or until cooked through and a skewer or knife inserted into the center comes out clean.

Meanwhile, put the sifted confectioners' sugar in a small bowl and slowly add just enough lemon juice, stirring as you go, to form a thick, smooth spreadable frosting.

Remove the cake from oven and transfer it from the pan onto a wire rack. Quickly drizzle or spread the cake with the frosting, sprinkle with hundreds and thousands, and let cool before serving.

Cardamom & mocha rice pudding

Rice pudding is always so comforting, and it's much loved in the Middle East, too. But I've come up with an altogether different flavor inspired by the rich and smooth cardamom-spiked coffee of the Arab world. Chocolate and coffee are a perfect pairing, especially in desserts, and this rich rice pudding makes a wonderfully indulgent beginning or end to any day.

SERVES 2 TO 4

½ cup short-grain rice

2¾ cups low-fat milk,
   or more if needed

1 teaspoon vanilla bean paste

½ teaspoon ground cinnamon

seeds from 3 fat cardamom pods,
   ground using a mortar and pestle

2 tablespoons of espresso or 1 heaped
   teaspoon brewed good-quality
   instant coffee

2 tablespoons superfine sugar

1¾oz dark chocolate (70% cocoa
   solids), coarsely chopped

¼ cup unsalted pistachio nuts, very
   finely blitzed in a food processor

Place a saucepan over very low heat, add all the ingredients, and stir vigorously to ensure the rice doesn't clump and that everything is well combined. Gently simmer the mixture, stirring regularly, for about 30 minutes until the rice is soft and cooked through. If it needs extra liquid, just add a little more milk.

Divide into 2 portions (if you're greedy like me), or 4 smaller portions for a more sensible treat, and serve.

Tahini cinnamon swirls

I love cinnamon in pastry and desserts. There really is no sweet treat that doesn't work with a little cinnamon in it, and these swirls have always been a favorite of mine. The tahini really enriches them, giving them a lovely nutty flavor that is something quite different and pleasing. They are great with coffee or served with vanilla ice cream. You can also freeze a whole roll of prepared pastry for later use, then cut and bake from frozen for an extra couple of minutes.

MAKES 12

1 x 11oz ready-rolled puff pastry sheet

¼ cup tahini (make sure it's not too thin, and avoid using excess oil)

3 tablespoons soft light brown sugar

2 teaspoons ground cinnamon

Preheat the oven to 400°F. Line a large baking pan with parchment paper.

Lay the pastry sheet on your work surface.

Mix the tahini with the sugar and cinnamon in a small bowl. Spread the mixture evenly all over the pastry sheet, leaving a clear border, ¾ inch wide, along one long edge. Starting from the opposite long edge, roll up the pastry tightly.

Cut the roll into 4, then cut each section into 3 equal slices. Lay the slices with the swirl facing up on the lined baking pan, spaced slightly apart, and flatten each one gently.

Bake for 20 to 22 minutes until nicely browned on top. Remove from the oven and let cool on the baking pan before serving.

Peanut butter & banana soft-serve

Every time I buy a bunch of bananas, inevitably one or two of them remain uneaten and end up ripening too much for my liking. And once you're tired of making banana bread, what do you do with them? Cut them into slices and pop them into the freezer, because this is one of the best ways I can think of to use them.

SERVES 2 TO 4

2 very ripe bananas, chopped and
    frozen solid

2 tablespoons smooth peanut butter

¼ cup heavy cream

½ teaspoon vanilla bean paste

¼ teaspoon ground cinnamon

Optional extras: ice cream cones
    or wafers, grated chocolate,
    toasted nuts

Remove the frozen bananas from the freezer and set aside for 5 minutes.

Put them into a food processor with the other main ingredients and blitz until smooth.

Serve immediately in dishes, topped with the chocolate and nuts if you wish, or serve in ice cream cones or layered between wafers.

Tahini & chocolate marmar cake

Store-bought *marmar* (marble) cake—soft, comforting, and delicious—was something I always adored as a kid. This recipe is my nod to that fantastic cake, which so many of us enjoyed while growing up.

SERVES 6 TO 8

4 eggs

¾ cup superfine sugar

1 teaspoon vanilla bean paste

⅓ cup heavy cream

½ cup unsalted butter, melted

1⅓ cups all-purpose flour

1 teaspoon baking powder

2 tablespoons unsweetened cocoa powder

2 tablespoons tahini

2 teaspoons sesame seeds

Preheat the oven to 350°F. Line a 2-pound (9-inch) loaf pan with a nonstick parchment paper liner, or cut a rectangle of parchment paper, crumple it up, then smooth it out and use it to line the pan.

Put the eggs, sugar, and vanilla bean paste into a mixing bowl and beat together until well combined. Mix in the cream, followed by the melted butter, mixing again until evenly combined. Add the flour and baking powder and mix thoroughly until you have a smooth batter.

Tip one-third of the batter into a separate bowl and set aside, then add the cocoa powder to the batter in the main bowl and mix until evenly incorporated.

Pour the chocolate batter into the lined pan. Drizzle the tahini all over the chocolate batter, and then pour the plain batter on top. Swirl a butter knife or fork handle gently through the batter to make a few swirly patterns, then sprinkle with the sesame seeds.

Bake the cake for 45 to 50 minutes, or until a skewer or knife inserted into the center comes out clean.

Remove from the oven, transfer the cake from the pan onto a wire rack, and let cool. Serve in slices.

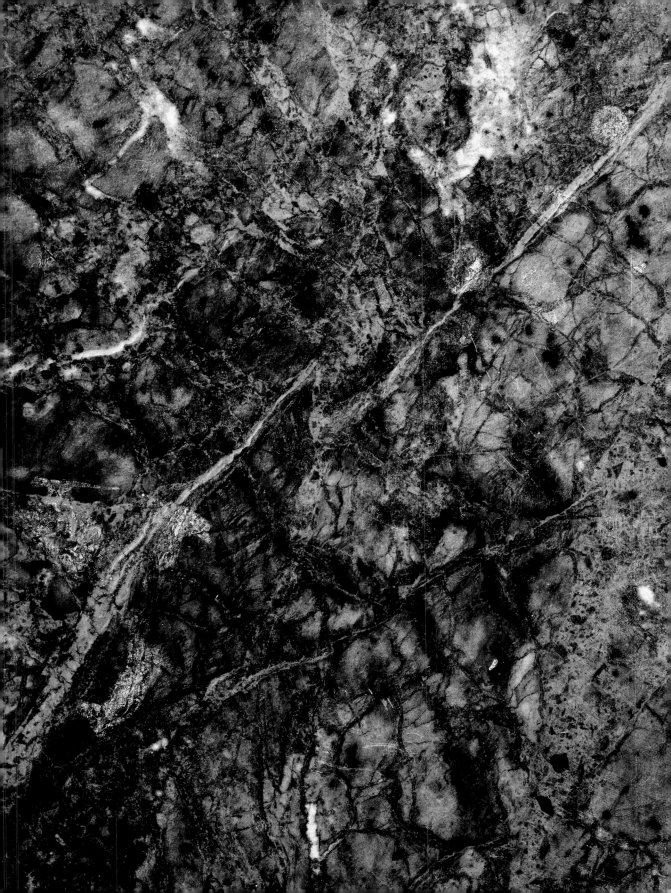

Index

Acknowledgments

To my mother and husband, I have to thank you first for putting up with me writing this book during a pandemic. I genuinely could not have done anything without leaning on you both for support, and you proved to be two incredibly solid pillars when my own foundations were a little unsteady. Thank you for bringing out the best in me and providing me with all I needed to produce a book of recipes that I am genuinely proud of.

To my brilliant agent, dear friend, and confidante Martine Carter—I still joke that you are the longest relationship I've ever had, and, if truth be told, I am so lucky to have your guidance and support in many areas of my life. I love and appreciate you very much. Thank you for all you do and for always trying to instill calm in me and keep me peaceful.

A huge thank you to Stephanie Jackson at Octopus Publishing—thank you for being a brilliant publisher, and friend, and for continuing to support my work and career. To the lovely Caroline Brown, publicity director at Octopus Publishing and your absolutely brilliant team, including Megan, Matt, Hazel, Victoria, and Charlotte, you're the best in the business, and, without fail, always do such amazing work to ensure my books do well. I couldn't be anywhere near as successful without all your hard work, planning, patience, and vision.

My brother from another mother, my photographer Kris Kirkham, what can I say that I haven't said so many times before about you? I absolutely love you with my whole heart, and thank God that I get to work (can you really call that kind of fun "work"?) with you and brilliant Eyder Rosso Goncalves, who is family to me too. You guys are everything to me and, yes, Eyder, when you eat almost all my shoot recipes, I know they're winners!

As always, one of the most unsung heroes in the process is my editor (and word alchemist) Sybella Stephens, who can take "Sabrina garble" and translate it beautifully into real English. Recipe writing is one thing, but editing recipe text to make sense is a whole other affair! Thank you for editing my words so beautifully and with such finesse.

To Jonathan Christie and my girl Jazzy "Fizzle" Bahra—thank you knocking it out of the park once again on the design front! Six books in and each time I know your task becomes more and more challenging, and with each book my profound respect for your work grows in so many ways. Thank you for being the best in the business.

And if you think my food looks good, please know that it has absolutely nothing to do with me and almost always everything to do with Laura Field—one of the most gifted, patient, and accommodating human beings I've ever known. Your food styling and guidance is invaluable and I literally couldn't imagine my books without your work in them. Thank you for always pulling it out of the bag and also bringing fantastic, happy, hard-working people to work on the shoots with you. Special thanks to Jessica McIntosh, Sarah Vassallo, and Hilary Lester, who assisted in cooking all the food so beautifully and who I am happy to call honorary Persians for their quick ability to perfect some incredibly precious, classic Persian recipes.

Behind the scenes, in the inner sanctum at Octopus HQ, I'd like to thank the incredible Kevin Hawkins for everything you do that puts my books on shelves everywhere… you really are a total guru! Thanks to Anna Bond and Denise Bates at Octopus Publishing for supporting this book and always making me feel so valued.

To everyone else at Octopus, I am so grateful for everything that you've done and continue to do for me. Thank you for creating and selling the most beautiful books with my name on them. I'm proud of every single one and really hope this one does you proud, too!

First published in Great Britain in 2022
by Aster, an imprint of Octopus Publishing Group Ltd
Carmelite House, 50 Victoria Embankment, London EC4Y 0DZ
www.octopusbooks.co.uk

An Hachette UK Company
www.hachette.co.uk

Distributed in the US by Hachette Book Group
1290 Avenue of the Americas, 4th and 5th Floors
New York, NY 10104

Distributed in Canada by Canadian Manda Group
664 Annette St., Toronto, Ontario, Canada M6S 2C8

ISBN 978 1 78325 514 6

Printed and bound in China
13 5 7 9 10 8 6 4 2

Publisher: Stephanie Jackson
Senior Managing Editor: Sybella Stephens
Copy Editor: Jo Richardson
Art Director: Jaz Bahra
Photographer: Kris Kirkham
Food Stylist: Laura Field
Props Stylist: Agathe Gits
Senior Production Manager: Peter Hunt

10/22